Lane With No Name

Other Books by Hilary Tham

Men & Other Strange Myths:
Poems & Art

Tigerbone Wine:
Poems

Paper Boats:
Poems of Hilary Tham

Lane With No Name

Memoirs & Poems of a
Malaysian-Chinese Girlhood

Hilary Tham

To Edith Ivins
With best wishes,

Fondly,

May 16, 1997

A THREE CONTINENTS BOOK
LYNNE RIENNER PUBLISHERS
BOULDER & LONDON

A Three Continents Book

Cover photograph of author by Rebecca SuYing Goldberg ©1996

Published in the United States of America in 1997 by
Lynne Rienner Publishers, Inc.
1800 30th Street, Boulder, Colorado 80301

and in the United Kingdom by
Lynne Rienner Publishers, Inc.
3 Henrietta Street, Covent Garden, London WC2E 8LU

Library of Congress Cataloging-in-Publication Data
Tham, Hilary, 1946–
    Lane with no name : memoirs & poems of a Malaysian-Chinese
    girlhood / Hilary Tham.
    ISBN 0-89410-830-1.—ISBN 0-89410-831-X (pbk.)
    1. Tham, Hilary, 1946– —Childhood and youth. 2. Women poets,
American—20th century—Biography. 3. Chinese—Malaysia—Social life
and customs. 4. Asian American women—Biography. 5. Chinese—
Malaysia—Poetry.   I. Title.
PS3570.H31837Z465 1997
811'.54—dc20
[B]   96-12899
                                                          CIP

British Cataloguing in Publication Data
A Cataloguing in Publication record for this book
is available from the British Library.

Printed and bound in the United States of America

    The paper used in this publication meets the requirements
⊗ of the American National Standard for Permanence of
    Paper for Printed Library Materials Z39.48-1984.

5 4 3 2 1

The idea of writing my memoirs goes against
the grain of my upbringing. Though I had breached
the taboo with my poems, prose
feels like a greater violation.

અ

This book is for my mother, Au LinTei,
a.k.a. Oo TuckKhoon, who raised me
to be an upright woman;

for my father, Tham SunHong,
who taught me to play;

and for my sisters, Su'en ChoyNgor and ChoyChoy,
my brothers, LeeLang and CheeLung,
and my sister, ChoyMui (I will remember you).

Contents

Photographs

Poems

Acknowledgments

The following chapters (sometimes in an earlier version) have appeared or are to appear in the publications listed below. Grateful acknowledgment is made to their editors and publishers:

"Before the Web," under the title "Raintree Seeds," was selected runner-up by *International Quarterly* personal essay judge Chaim Potok in its 1995 competition and was published in *International Quarterly*, Fall 1995. "The Nuns" appeared in *Potomac Review*; "Chickens" appeared in *Palo Alto Review*; "The Soy Sauce Compound" appeared in *Excursus*; and "The Corner Coffee House" in *Doubletake*.

These poems have appeared in the following publications and in collections of my poems: "Moving Up" in *Metropolitain*; "Grandfather's Favoritism" in *Hungry As We Are*, the *Washington Writers' Publishing House Anthology*; and "May Means Beautiful in Chinese" in *Gargoyle*.

My thanks and love to Isaac Goldberg, my father-in-law, for patient and most helpful proofreading of the manuscript. To my husband, Joe, whose rocklike presence in my life gives me strength, I can only say (with British restraint) the usual, "You know, terribly fond of you and all that, old chap."

Prologue

My first sight of America as our airplane neared New York was the green lady holding her torch above the blue waters of the Atlantic. "There, there's the Statue of Liberty!" my husband said, possessive pride in his voice. My husband, Joe, was American. He was twenty-five and I was twenty-four. We had met while he was serving in the Peace Corps in my home country, Malaysia. He was certain I was going to love America. It was not a case of love at first sight.

When we stood outside the airport, Joe took deep breaths of the crisp cold autumn air, said, "It's good to be home!" I was shivering with cold, I was freezing in 60 degrees Fahrenheit, and I was homesick. Everything, the dry air and the people with black or white skin, their voices, their words were alien to me. I was a woman who had grown up in hot, humid, equatorial rain forests, among people of color, varying shades of brown, who spoke Malay, Chinese, Tamil, English. But not English rendered unrecognizable by New York accents. I was scared—scared at the prospect of the future in a strange town in a strange country, in a strange climate. By my side was the man I loved but who was, I realized with sudden clarity, almost as unknown as the land I was to call home the rest of my life.

I wrapped my arms about me and looked at the people in their thin coats and light jackets hurrying past. None of them seemed to notice the cold. I knew then that the cotton shirts, skirts, and sandals

1

in my bags were as inadequate as I for this new climate and this new life.

The tall, uniformed customs officer, a black woman with teeth white as a toothpaste advertisement, had been friendly. "Welcome to America. Anything to declare?" she asked, chalk in hand poised above my suitcase. "No, nothing to declare," Joe answered for us. Nothing except guilt, my mind said silently. In following my heart, I had left my family and abandoned my family obligations. My mother had wept at the airport in Subang Jaya, Malaysia, from fears and uncertainties besetting her; uncertain when, if ever, she would see me again, uncertain how she would manage to hold household and educate the three younger children since I, her second child and second source of income for the family, was leaving, without certainty of employment or ability to send money home. My husband was returning to graduate school on a fellowship; we would not be able to send her aid for quite some years. She would have to depend entirely on my older brother to be filial and fiscally responsible.

My first years in the United States were a constant adjustment of expectations to realities, of revising Asian customs to assimilate American ones. I had been raised in a rigid society where one's behavior was dictated by birth order and family position. From the age of five, a Chinese child is taught its place and the responsibilities of that place within the family hierarchy. At meals, I learned to set the table and to wait for permission to eat. It became second nature to always invite my grandmother and parents to eat their rice and wait for them to lift their chopsticks and rice-bowls before I could touch mine. I learned the proper tone of voice (respectful always) and the correct words to use in speaking to my elders. I learned not to say what I thought. Children were expected to be respectfully silent and to listen to their elders (and betters) always, but especially at mealtimes. Parents did not ask about their child's day or doings; it was assumed the child was dutiful and studying hard at school. The one thing that no one ever talked about was feelings. It was not so much that Malaysians respected emotional privacy as the unspoken belief that individuality must be subjugated to the communal good. To speak of personal feelings was to put one's desires ahead of being a quietly working cog of the family, the clan; it was regarded with horror, like a cancerous cell in a wholesome body.

The one national characteristic of Americans I found most disconcerting was their direct, up-front assumption of psychological intimacy. Unlike Asians (and Europeans, I found later), Americans give you a lot of physical space. Perhaps this stems from the vastness of the country. There is space to spare. I have observed this in supermarket check-out lines, queues to board buses, trains, planes. At parties, Americans talk to you and each other with a foot or two of airspace between your faces. But they will open up their hearts and tell the most intimate details of their lives, even to strangers. Asians and Europeans move in physically on you when they talk—they breathe into your face while they converse about politics, culture, the weather—they talk about anything except themselves and their feelings. It may be that, living in small, crowded countries, they are more accustomed to being squashed up bodily against each other and compensate by maintaining mental and emotional distances as an automatic reflex for survival.

As a child, it had been impressed on me that we must be constantly aware of the importance of "face," the mask we present to the world—how we must always be careful to "give face" and "save face." It is part of the social imperative: the obligation to help one another keep intact the appearance of dignity; of self, of family, of clan and race. We have an unspoken contract with each other to keep doors tightly closed on family skeletons. The idea of writing my memoirs goes against the grain of my upbringing. Though I had breached the taboo with my poems, prose feels like a greater violation.

Living in America has been a constant process of learning a new culture, adjusting to and evaluating the new culture vis-à-vis the old. It has been like being in a buffet-style restaurant, with tables loaded with a smorgasbord of choices where I had always eaten at a fixed table with a set menu: Select A or A. I love the American bone-deep belief that anyone can be anything if you work hard at it and do not quit on your dream. That not pursuing the dream is a disgrace; failure to achieve is not. This concept is the most liberating and empowering gift America has given me. Without embracing this ideology, I could never have written about the real faces behind the preserved faces of my life, my family, and my people.

The Tham family in 1971, at the time of my marriage.
Sitting (L to R): Chak SiewLan (LeeLang's wife),
Mother Au LinTei, Grandmother Tham née Lau LinSong,
Father Tham SunHong, and older brother LeeLang;
standing (L to R): younger sister Su'en ChoyNgor,
younger brother CheeLung, my husband Joe Goldberg,
myself, and younger sister ChoyChoy.

1
Before the Web

My two brothers ran free in abandoned fields of *lallang* (tall wild grass with cutting edges) near our house. Their kites flapping in the air behind them, they joined the neighborhood boys in the windy season, when boys' minds gloated over slashing and cutting loose other boys' kites. I had to stay in and do women's work, washing clothes, ironing, helping care for my baby sisters.

Trees were forbidden to me. Girls did not climb trees.

When I demanded to ride a bicycle (my older brother had taught me secretly), mother gave reluctant permission and warned me to mount and dismount with care lest I tear my hymen and be branded a non-virgin on my wedding night. Proof of virginity was a Chinese husband's right. She told me a story of a bride from the old village in Guangdong—a tomboy bride who was sent back to her home in disgrace. Her family had to return the dowry and the poor girl eventually threw herself into the village well. Mother recalled how my paternal grandmother had given my father a white cotton kerchief on the wedding night and demanded to see it first thing the next morning. Luckily my mother had not destroyed her hymen by tomboyish activities and the kerchief was satisfactorily scarlet. Grandmother Tham, who opposed the match, would have been pleased to have a valid excuse to send the bride packing. Father had bypassed her matriarchal authority: he had chosen a bride for himself. Grandmother would have been delighted if his choice had failed the test.

My mother was fourteen when my father sent a matchmaker to her parents. The year was 1942 and World War II had come to Malaya (it became Malaysia in 1963). On December 10th, 1941, Japanese troops had seized Singapore from the British and sunk two British battleships off the coast of Kelantan. People were terrified at the prospect of Japanese occupation. Rumors said that young virgins would be forced to become "comfort women" and to service soldiers. During the Japanese occupation (1942–1945), many young women hacked off their hair and darkened their faces and hands with shoe polish to avoid the fate of being dragged away as "mistresses." My mother's parents had rejected a proposed match six months earlier because she was too young, but fear of the Japanese made them eager to accept the new match. When the matchmaker brought my father for the viewing, Mother's parents told her it was time for her to wed and asked if she liked this man, Tham SunHong.

My father was twenty-two then. He was slim, with good features, a high nose, sparkling eyes, and a ready smile. He seemed nice, so she said "yes." How could she know that her "yes" meant the end of peaceful days, of being loved and cherished and spoiled by her parents, that she thus committed herself to a life of discord, infidelities with other women, infectious gonorrhea, grief, debts, lies, a constant struggle to "save face"?

My father had a little more freedom and choice in matrimony. The matchmaker, Old Man KimKee, showed him a collection of photographs of suitable girls precipitated into the marriage brokerage by the Japanese invasion. Father picked mother's photograph out of a score of others.

My mother still has that photograph. It is a black-and-white studio portrait. She is, here, a thirteen-year-old, slender in a white dress, a sweet-faced child with large, serious eyes, curly black hair (perms were in) loose on her shoulders, standing in front of a giant spiderweb—a studio prop of white string popular at the time. Looking at it now, I think how symbolic that picture was—the young girl I never knew, flat chest bearing only the promise of womanhood, her life and dreams as whole and as fragile as the gossamer-seeming web behind her.

Mother remembers being kept home from school by her parents when Japanese troops occupied the town. Her mother hacked off her newly permed hair and hid her in their room, warned her not to look out the window. She was allowed to come downstairs for meals. Her wedding picture shows her with a boy's haircut.

To marry her, my father had to obtain his widowed mother's permission. At that time, young people did not question, much less flout, tradition. One did not marry without parental consent. The cornerstone of a Chinese wedding was the kowtowing (kneeling and bowing the head to the floor) before the parents and offering cups of hot *cha*, tea. There was no marriage if the tea was not accepted and sipped ceremonially. When concubines, secondary wives, were brought home, tea had to be offered to the parents and the first wife. If she rejected it, the union was null and void. The new woman did not attain secondary-wife status, remaining a mere mistress, a loose woman; and her children, illegitimate, could not inherit.

Mother warned us girls to always be alert and not let our future husbands sneak a concubine into the family. We heard the story of a relative, Cousin Leng, many times: how she was tricked into validating her husband's second wife, one hot afternoon when a strange woman thrust a teacup at her as she emerged from a long sit in the bathroom and Cousin Leng took the cup before she realized what it meant.

Malaysian law was changed in the early 1970s; the Chinese custom of concubinage is no longer permitted. Muslim men are allowed four wives, according to the national religion of Islam. Non-Muslim men are limited to one wife at a time, a legacy of British colonization, and must divorce her before taking a second woman to wife.

When my father showed the matchmaker's photograph of Mother to his mother, our grandmother said, "No. The girl is too scrawny to bear sons. Find a healthier, fatter girl." Father argued with her for days and finally threatened to run away to a temple and become a monk. "If I can't marry this girl, you will never carry grandsons in your arms." His mother yielded.

I think, given modern circumstances now prevalent even in Malaysia, my parents' marriage would have had a chance to be happy. But their union was set in the unyielding matrix of Chinese tradition that decreed that newlyweds must live with the man's family, subject to the rule, orders, and whims of their elders. In everything but name, the bride became her mother-in-law's slave-girl.

My father worked as a sales clerk in the hardware store that belonged to a rich cousin of his late father. He and his mother (and after the wedding, my mother) lived in two rooms of the rambling clan house at the end of Meru Road in the town of Kelang, five miles from the town of Port Swettenham. The port town is now named Port Kelang, part of the movement in the 1970s to remove vestiges of British colonization.

Grandmother promptly flexed her matriarchal muscles. She ordered the new bride about all day long, setting her lists of chores: chop wood for cookfires, feed the chickens and ducks, plant the tapioca patch, enlarge the vegetable garden, wash the floors of the clan house. Mother says the tapioca patch was a godsend—when the Japanese occupation was at its worst, when they had to eat the leaves off the *nangka* (jackfruit) and pomelo trees and boil bark for beverages, the tapioca tubers were the only thing they had to give their stomachs a feeling of fullness.

Grandmother Tham was jealous of her only son's bride and would sit with them constantly, glaring at the girl who was now the focus of her son's attentions.

"In the beginning," my mother would recall, "your father used to take me out to a movie or to a restaurant, and we would buy a package of lo-mein to take home to his mother." Grandmother refused to eat the noodles on the pretext she was too sleepy when they returned. The next noon, when her son was at work, she would throw the noodles into the trash pile, rant at her daughter-in-law for making her son neglect her, and forbid my mother to go out again.

Night after night, Grandmother sat between my young parents in the hall, telling my father news and gossip of relatives as he tried to converse with his silent ("shy," he thought) bride. He did not realize that his bride's monosyllabic answers to his questions and her refusals to go out with him (on the pretext of tiredness) were related to the scared glances she gave his glowering mother. He was used to his mother's grumpiness. He claims now that it never occurred to him that his child-bride was terrified of his tiny, wrinkled old mother. He had never feared his mother. He had always gotten his way with her; he knew she would scream and scold and then say "yes" to him. That was the pattern of their relationship.

My father was not a patient man. He soon grew tired of trying to draw out his pretty child-bride, tired of sitting in a dimly lit hall watching moths kamikazeing on the kerosene lamp. He tired of listening to the mosquitoes humming in the jungle surrounding the house, the rustle of cheap cigarette paper as his mother rolled herself another smoke, and later, the hiss of water meeting fire as she tossed her butt-end into the spittoon at her feet. He was young, eager for fun and companionship and adventures. He wanted to stroll in the town center, with his pretty wife smiling adoringly at him. Instead, he had a mouse of a girl who would not look at him, who hardly spoke at all, who submitted to him like a rag doll in the dark privacy of their bedroom. Raised with the freedom that was the birthright of any Chinese male, how could he know that she was trapped in the dictates of Chinese tradition—her mother had impressed on her that good women did not display unseemly enjoyment of "mingling" (the Chinese term for sex, until the English language came along with a word they took over. Now, *sexi* is the preferred Chinese word for sex).

I gather, from something my mother once said to me later in life, that she did learn the pleasures of sex: "We women are so weak. Let a man place his hand on our breast and our bones turn to water." And another time, she said, "There were times when we were very happy together, when he was loving and kind to me." These times usually coincided with the periods when my grandmother took a job with a relative and went away for a month, sometimes even a year. I remember my mother sewing two new dresses and taking dancing lessons the year I was ten. She learned the waltz, the fox-trot, and the cha-cha for a trip with my father to the island resort of Penang. They were acting as chaperons for a rich cousin dating a wealthy friend of Father's. They went to nightclubs and they danced to dreamy music in darkened rooms filled with smoke and potted palms. They danced as the singer in the band sang huskily in Cantonese, "*Dim kai ngo choon yi ley? Yan wai ley hai lang* . . . Why do I love you? Because you are so fair." This is the one Cantonese song I know by heart; my mother sang it around the house for weeks after the trip. Later, she told me those four days were forever special, for it was the only time he had treated her like a person instead of just a wife. The Penang trip was the high point of her romance-starved life.

That was just after his mistress of ten years had married another man and before he fell in love with a new woman.

Grandmother Tham

My mother
at age 13

Wedding photo,
1943:
Father is 22,
Mother 14.

Grandmother Tham

11

*Father playing
the saxophone*

*My parents in Penang,
four happy days*

*Father as female lead
in a Chinese opera*

2

The Soy Sauce Compound

I was born in the house of the Soy Sauce Compound. Mother said it was just after the British came back to Malaya and the Japanese occupation troops moved out. I remember little of my first home, only the waa-hoo-whoop-hoop-hoo-ing of gibbons in the jungle behind the house in the cool of mornings. And the huge coffin in Grandmother's room. She used it as a table sometimes for her clothes but always cleared them off when Grand-Uncle Three came to collect the rent. It was his coffin. I remember little else. The house and yard are gone now, erased by bulldozers and new housing estates. "Why do we refer to the house as the Soy Sauce Compound, or Soy Sauce Yard?" I asked.

Brother remembers . . .

I guess they called it the Soy Sauce Compound because Soy Sauceman Leong lived there in the house with us. He made soy sauce in the yard. He had huge vats of smelly beans rotting and oozing brown sauce. The whole yard smelled, the house too.

    We lived there until I was six and you were four. I remember the house very clearly. It was L-shaped. Our parents and us kids shared one of the two rooms to the left of the front hall. Sauceman Leong and his wife and two daughters had the other room. Across the hall was Grandmother's room, where Grand-Uncle Three kept his coffin. Grandmother had a narrow iron bed squeezed between the wall and the coffin. She was not afraid of the coffin. It gave me the shakes. Especially after the night Grandmother had a fight with Father and climbed into the coffin. She hung a noose around her neck and screamed and howled, tore at her hair until it hung over her face and she looked like a malignant ghost. I can see it still, her face all twisted up, her mouth a dark hole sending out horrible noises, her neck and noose just visible above the edge of the coffin.

There was another coffin in the house. It was in the room between Sauceman's in-laws' room and the kitchen. I never went in that room. I saw the coffin when they went in to get wood for cooking from that room.

The bathroom was a small shed off the kitchen. Further away from the house was the outhouse. It was a lean-to shack with four-foot-high walls of flimsy planks, enclosing a deep pit. There was a pair of two-by-four wood pieces over the pit. You had to be very careful where you placed your feet or you would fall in. When the pit got full, they dug another and moved the shack over the new pit. It was a portable outhouse.

I remember a pond and the rows and rows of earthenware jars Sauceman Leong used. The smell of soybeans was pretty awful. I never played there in the afternoons because the flies came then; they clustered all over the rims of the jars and the heated smell of fermenting beans made it hard to breathe.

Behind the house were jungle and rubber trees with lots of monkeys. The grown-ups made a monkey trap once. They dug a pit under the trees and set a trapdoor to fall down over it when the bait, a bunch of bananas, was moved. They caught a monkey and ate him. For days after that, crowds of angry monkeys perched in the trees and hooted and screamed at the house. I watched from the hall window. I was afraid they'd snatch me and eat me for revenge.

Mother remembers . . .

Your brother remembers well. Everyone called it the Soy Sauce Compound because of Sauceman Leong; he's dead now. He rented two rooms in the house and the compound was filled with his vats of fermenting soybeans. Sauceman Leong made good soybean paste and sauce. He made a good living from that all his life. Unlike our miserable attempts to go into business.

I remember the time we started an oil press in the compound. Nearer the house than the sauce jars. We bought copra, dried coconut meat, a shredder, and a simple oil press, the kind you pushed a long pole handle around in a circle to turn a giant screw which pressed the oil out of the shredded coconut. We hired a Malay boy from Meru *kampong* (village) to pedal the wheel to turn the shredder. Your grand mother and I, we worked the oil press. The first time we took our oil to market, the Chinese gangsters, the collaborators, they took all our sales money for "tea money." We had to let them or the Japanese soldiers would have come and thrown us in jail or chopped off a hand for not having a permit to press oil.

Next, your father and grandmother decided to make money by producing animal feed. There was a shortage and it was fetching high prices. We bought a lorry-load of tapioca, spent days shredding it—the coconut shredder came in useful here—raked it out on burlap sacks to dry in the sun. It was hard work. Anxious afternoons. Every time a cloud appeared in the sky, we'd look to see if there was light under it or dark. Dark cloud feet meant rain and we had to run around collecting all the shredded tapioca into heaps and cover them. Once the cloud or rain had gone, we had to rake and spread the tapioca out again. How my arms and legs ached every night, as if my bones had turned to powder. Finally, all the tapioca was dried. By then, there was a tapioca glut. Everyone had been making tapioca animal feed, like us. We got a very low price. We lost money again.

The last business your father tried was the ice cream stall at the town playground. He and Grandmother sold my dowry—gold, my chains, bracelets, and earrings—and bought the stall and ice cream–making equipment. Nobody realized it was the beginning of the monsoon season. It rained without stopping all week long. We didn't have a freezer. They ended up giving away their snow cones and ice cream to the kids at the end of each day. Your father gave up his dream of being his own boss and went back to work in Grand-Uncle Three's hardware store across the river.

No, no. Your brother is wrong. We never moved the outhouse. The original pit was so deep, it never got even halfway full. The worms in the pit bottom took care of that.

Your brother was so shocked by your grandmother's climbing

into the coffin with a noose that he fell sick and ran a high fever for three days. Your grandmother was like that; she threw a fit whenever she couldn't get her way. She was poorly brought up, not house-trained. I was frightened of the coffin at first but I got used to it. Grand-Uncle Three used to hide his stockpile of rice noodles in his coffin during the war. Luckily the Japanese troops never came to the house. They only did house searches in the town. Not that we kept the food long; Grand-Uncle's family ate it up in a few months.

They were very fond of monkey meat, Sauceman Leong and his in-laws, Old Man Seng and Old Woman Seng. Also your father. And your grandmother. They were always talking about how to catch another monkey. I never ate the monkeys they caught and cooked. Your grandmother was skilled at slaughtering monkeys. I didn't watch her do it. Those monkeys were very much like people. Actually, they were the white-faced gibbons with the long faces and sad-looking eyes. They were very smart and seemed to have almost human sense. One time, I scolded one of them for urinating on my drying tapioca and he scurried away. The next thing I knew, my hair was dripping wet. That monkey had sneaked into a tree above me and was peeing on my head. Those monkeys were very naughty!

Father remembers . . .

I had a pet monkey when we lived at the Sauce Yard. I found him as a baby; something must have happened to his mother. I hand-fed him until he could eat by himself. He was certainly a clever little thing. One morning, my wallet fell out of my pocket into our well and he climbed down and got it back for me. I was very fond of him.

That false friend Leong, that soy sauce seller, he and his in-laws asked my mother if they could have my pet monkey for dinner when I was away for a month. My unnatural mother said "Yes." She even slaughtered the poor little thing for them. She was probably wanting to eat it herself, before the others suggested it. I'm as fond of monkey stew as anyone else, but to kill and eat my pet monkey! That woman had no softness in her heart.

Your grandmother was not a good mother. She abandoned me, left me to sleep on the floors of relatives' shops all the time. Once, she left me at the Kelang shop for a whole day and no one offered me any meals. Finally, at closing time, the cook saw me in the corner and gave me the crust from the rice pot, softened in hot water. That was the most delicious meal of my life. To this day, I still love to eat rice crust in hot water.

My father was a sullen man; he hardly spoke to me when my mother left me in his care. I would watch him as he sat hunched over his sewing machine, stitching mosquito netting and mattress covers. I hoped he'd notice me, speak a kind word to me. He was sickly, always hacking and coughing, rubbing at his crotch. He caught syphilis, whoring in Singapore, when he first came to Malaya. They took me back to Hong Kong when I was nine, back to his father's house. My father died there. Not of syphilis. That got cured. Tuberculosis. My mother disappeared. Two years later, she came by and had a huge screaming fight with my grandfather. After she left, he threw me out of his house.

I didn't know what to do after my grandfather told me to leave his house, he never wanted to see my mother or me again. I didn't know where my mother had gone. I did not want to go to her. She would only beat me. She beat me when I almost drowned at six, the time I was caught by a flash flood in my first monsoon in Malaya. She beat me when I fell out of a tree. She beat me any time she noticed me. I went to Grand-Uncle Two. He said, "What are you doing here?" but he took me in. He was kind; he sent me to school and bought me a set of school clothes and a Boy Scout's uniform. In winter, when I washed my school uniform, it didn't always dry in time. The next morning, I had to wear it damp to school. I loved being in the Boy Scouts. Those were the happiest two years of my life.

Six months before high-school graduation, my mother came, like an evil spirit, and took me to Malaya again. She said it was time I earned a living and began to support her. My heart felt so dead then. But she was my mother and I had to obey. I never knew she was not my real mother, that I was a bought child, until I was forty, when my wife told me what the relatives told her when she married me. I've been a filial son, though my mother didn't deserve it.

I've never been afraid of hard work or anything. I used to smuggle luxury goods, scented bath soaps, cloth, hair cream, between Kelang and Kuala Lumpur. Twenty-three miles uphill and downhill in the dark, through rubber plantations. I pedaled my old clunky bicycle with its little dynamo headlight. The rubber trees with their carved sap patches looked like tall Indians in white *dhoti* skirts. A Japanese patrol caught me once. Luckily I was on my way back and had no illegal goods on me. The soldiers wanted to know why I was out after curfew. I had picked up some Japanese and told them some story about being in love and needing to see my girl-friend. They were young soldiers; they told me to go home, to wait for sunrise, and then they let me go. I heard them laughing out loud as I pedaled home. Me, I laughed silently all the way home.

Coffins? There was a coffin. The one in your grandmother's room. Grand-Uncle Three's coffin. He was a sickly old man. In the end, he didn't get to use it. He died in his shop-house on the other side of the river the week after the British bombed the bridge. It was the only bridge. There was no way to get the coffin to him or him to the coffin. His sons buried him in a makeshift box. They saved the coffin for later use by their mother.

Your brother is right. There was a second coffin. Cousin Lo's father's coffin. He was a quiet man. I had completely forgotten about his coffin until now. I don't even remember when he died. After the war, I think. I know he got to use his coffin, because he was buried in it.

I don't believe in worrying about the future or the afterlife. Look at Grand-Uncle Three! All his planning came to nothing. It would have been better for him if he had eaten more roast duck and green ginger beef noodles with the money.

Days later, I was still processing the memories shared, talking about the Soy Sauce Compound. This was the first time Father had talked so much and in such detail about his parents and his forma-tive years. Though he often entertained us as children with anec-dotes and jokes, he had avoided speaking of his youth. Even Mother thought he had come to Malaya at age eleven and did not know he had been brought back and forth from Hong Kong like a yo-yo ball on a string since he was six years old.

This new information answered a lot of questions I had asked myself as I grew and moved from pure adoration of the father who was always a delight to be with, the man who playfully tousled my hair on his way out to a party every evening, to a disappointed acceptance that he was a libertine, who lived only for "good times, loose women, and sentimental songs," a man who had never saved a cent for a down payment on a house or for his children's education.

A puppet jerked around by his mother, a woman widowed early and with her own set of problems, mainly financial and temperamental, my father learned too early that he was powerless, unable to control his life, dependent on the whim of strangers for even just rice crust for a meal. The subsequent failures with establishing a business during the war must have driven the lesson home. I was reminded of a Jewish friend, the child of Holocaust survivors. She told me her parents constantly emphasized the uncertainty of life, how any night or day, heavy-booted troops could come and take them away from all they had, all they loved, all they knew. All her adult life, she had been unable to plan beyond a week at a time, unable to save money. There was the fear it was all for naught. It would all be taken from her. So she spent, with irrational urgency, on every pleasure, food, paintings, music, for this she knew: no one could strip past joys from her. They were vanished, existing only in memory, and safe from ruthless, all-powerful hands.

Subconsciously, my father must have arrived at this philosophy for himself. So he savored every moment he could, certain that at any moment, power in the form of an angry mother, a collaborator, a soldier, or an evil spirit would appear and force him to leave everything he loved and come along. Having gone hungry so often in his youth, his chief focus is food these last years of his life. With terminal kidney failure, aware the knock on the door is imminent, he wants to eat favorite dishes every two hours. We used to laugh at the speed he emptied his rice bowl in the past, not knowing his childhood insecurities of being removed at any instant by his "Jack-in-the-Box" mother. He still crams food into his mouth as if he has a train to catch. But we cannot laugh anymore.

Moving Up

Mother lied to Father for years to save
from the housekeeping money a down-payment
on a house with attap-thatch roof and packed
mud floor. Then she moved us there in a pedicab.
Father stayed behind and sulked in the tiny
room with use-of-kitchen we had rented for
five cramped years. The landlady, with eight
families renting in her ten room house,
talked him into joining us a week later.

He told us to remember his great sacrifice.
In his mind, two bedrooms and home-ownership
did not compare to a crowded cement floor.
A year later, thanks to Mother's magic
with housekeeping money, we achieved cement
for the floor and tin for the roof.

Security for me as a child was listening
to rain pattering on that tin roof, squeezed
in a bed with all my siblings. Even then,
I began to yearn, as my mother must have
yearned, for a little privacy, my own space.

—from *Men & Other Strange Myths*

3

Lane with No Name

When I was five, Mother bought a house for seven hundred dollars and moved us there. Our new home was the end unit of a row of wooden houses on a laterite dirt lane with no name branching off Meru Road. The orange dirt lane began with a bridge over the Meru Road monsoon drain and ran beside a subsidiary drain past our row up to a small wooden temple and a raggle-taggle group of squatters' shacks on the edge of the jungle. Dominating our view from the lane was the Kelang (Boys) High School, which my brothers attended. Next to the school's playing fields was a long hill given to the Chinese dead in the front and Christian dead in the rear, with a small church tucked among them. The Chinese graves near the road were the oldest: huge cement-covered mounds with tall marble markers. Most of the graves had a lithographed photo of the dead person inhabiting it. None of them ever smiled. They all looked fierce and grim. I was afraid of the cemetery. Grand-Uncle One's tall brick mansion on Meru Road faced the middle of the cemetery. Whenever I had to go there, I walked as fast as I could and never looked behind me. I was convinced that to show awareness or fear would cause a hovering, hostile ghost to grab me. Like the ostrich, my reasoning had a childish logic: if I pretended ghosts did not exist, they would, with equal courtesy, pretend I did not exist for them.

The tiny temple at the end of our nameless lane was dedicated to the Empress of Heaven, Tin Hau. She was not a popular goddess, unlike Kwan Yin, the Goddess of Mercy, who had the huge stone temple on two acres of land on Meru Road. Her temple had triple halls of worship, gardens of flowers with walkways, long white-washed balustrade walls, and companies of real nuns and monks who chanted prayers to her all day long. The temple on our lane had one hall of worship and a small yard. It was owned and run by an *Ah Por* (Old Grandma) and her son. However, it was holy enough for our ordinary needs—I remember when Grandfather Au died, Uncle Yuen went down the lane in the dark and bought holy water to wash his face before burial. When I was seven, Mother took me there to have my ears ritually pierced.

The house we moved into when I was five was actually an illegal add-on by an enterprising squatter. When Mother bought it from him for seven hundred *ringgit* (dollars), which represented more than a year's pay for Father, she and Father had a huge fight over it. He said, "Only fools waste their money on houses." I believe he was upset because he resented her having saved that much from the meager housekeeping money he gave her when he had empty pockets at the end of each month. Mother said he treated money like fresh fruit—very perishable and to be used as soon as possible.

I remember arriving at the house the first time in a pedicab. The house seemed grand to me. There was a front hall for a living room, a narrow passage with two bedrooms, a kitchen, and a room for bathing. And they were all ours; we did not have to share them, like we did when we rented rooms, with multiple families. The out-house at the back was a communal one and was one of two shared by the row of neighbors.

Though the house only had rough plank walls, an *attap*-thatch roof, and a packed mud floor, we were happy. There were six of us then, Grandmother who slept on a sofa in the hall, my parents, my older brother and our younger sister, ChoyMui, who died a year later, and myself. We kids were pleased to have a room to ourselves. Then there was the out-of-doors for us to claim.

There was a *saga* tree (rain tree) which dropped bright scarlet seeds for us to play jacks with. There was a young guava tree, beside the outhouse, with yellow flowers promising fruit later. Mother built a henhouse under it and raised chickens for egg money. Best of all, there was a vast empty lot on the other side of our lane with tall grasses, dotted purple and pink with wildflowers. In later years, my brothers flew kites with the neighborhood boys there. They caught fighting spiders in the bushes. They crawled about in the monsoon drain looking for mud-suckers and catfish.

The girls had more sedate games: we picked purple button-flowers and played tug-of-war, using the flower heads to engage and their stalks as rope. We picked frangipani flowers from the trees by the temple. We tied a bunch together with a rubber band and played "Keep it in the air with your foot."

My favorite weed was the *mimosa*. It had pretty pink flowers, like dandelion puffballs. When you touched them, your hands came away dusted with golden and pink pollen. The best part about *mimosa* was its sensitive leaves. I'd stroke a rachis of leaflets with a finger or a stalk of grass. Sometimes, I merely breathed hard on it. Pair by pair, the sensitive leaves folded together and shrank down and away, as if to hide from me. The *malu-malu* (shy) plant, as the Malays called it, could be found in clumps all over the field. The cowherd's cows, which grazed there in the early evenings, left them alone as *mimosa* had prickles on its stems.

Our mud floor was covered with cement by Grandfather Au, who mixed it himself and laid down a surface so smooth it was the envy of the neighbors. Several years later, Mother had saved enough to replace the *attap* roof with a zinc roof and we did not have to endure mouse droppings falling on our heads and on our homework anymore. Still later, Mother had the house wired for electricity. Then she built an addition herself with Grandfather's help. She added a third bedroom and a dining room. But we gained only the use of the dining room; she rented the new bedroom out to a working couple.

Father warned Mother each time she improved the house. "You're wasting your effort. You're pouring my money down the drain. This house is illegal. The government can take it away from you, tear it down, any time they want." Mother ignored him and went to file another application at the District Office. Finally, the District Officer, a friendly, soft-spoken Malay man, came. He knocked on the walls, inspected our electric outlets and wires, climbed onto the roof, smiled at the shine on the cement floor, and accepted a cup of tea. Mother was extremely excited and hopeful after he left. "He drank my tea! If he was going to reject my application, he wouldn't have done that, would he?"

A few months later, a different man came and nailed an aluminum plate with the house number "188-A" over our front door.

The legitimate house that our house was built onto was number 188. We had achieved a sub-number; we had achieved recognition of our right to exist. Mother was so jubilant she made egg noodles and wonton soup for dinner, a treat she made only for birthday celebrations. "I told you so, I told you so!" she laughed as she recounted all the fears, hopes, struggles, things she had done, to arrive at this happy day. Father said, "Fool's luck! That's what it is. You've used up a lot of luck today. Better not gamble on anything else."

4

Family Labels

Arithmetic

For 24 years, I was plainer than plain,
passable, Mother said. These 18 years
your hands and lips tell me I am beautiful.
Perhaps in another 6 years, it will balance
and I will believe you.

—from *Tigerbone Wine*

My parents brought us up with labels. Each child was tagged with "good" and "bad" labels, the former to build a sense of self-worth, the latter to keep us humble. There was enough truth in the labels attached to each child to keep us honest with ourselves. Each child was told his or her good and bad characteristics early and often.

LeeLang (Eldest Son) was hard-working, sensible, and dependable, but not clever.

ChoyKam (I, Second Child and Eldest Daughter) was intelligent, brave, and talented but indolent, impertinent, and not pretty.

ChoyMui (Second Daughter) died before she got labeled.

CheeLung (Second Son) was brilliant and eloquent but bad-tempered, clumsy, and stubborn.

27

ChoyNgor (Third Daughter) was beautiful and intelligent but sulky and disobedient.

ChoyChoy (Last Daughter) was obedient, diligent, and sunny in nature, but not clever.

Sometimes, I wonder what each of us might have achieved if we had not been made so aware of our limitations. I do not know how I would have coped with a label of being "not clever," meaning stupid. Children always seize on the worst interpretation of a word. I was never told I was ugly, only "not pretty," but I knew it meant I was as ugly as a baboon. I'd look in the mirror and, on bad days, could detect how my receding forehead, flat nose, and jutting lower face did resemble a gibbon's. This probably affected my lifelong belief that marriage was not an option in my future. I attributed it to my being a pessimist about happy marriages from my parents' example.

I envied my older brother. Where my parents were concerned, it seemed my brother could do no wrong and I could do no right. When we presented our report cards, he got "Well done" for his B's and C's while I got "You can do better than this" for my B's and A's. I protested this. "You're not fair! I got better grades than LeeLang." Our parents' usual reply knocked more nails into our self-image coffins. "Your brother is not as clever as you are. He is doing his best. You, on the other hand, can get all A's if you tried. You need to study harder; no man is going to marry you for your looks."

My parents claimed they loved us equally, and rewarded us with praise in proportion to our efforts. My paternal grandmother made no effort to disguise her partiality for the boys in the family. Elder Brother was given an egg for breakfast. She'd heap meat (when we had it) on his rice. Because he was the Boy. She wanted to favor my younger brother, CheeLung, also, but he foiled her attempts. He'd share his goodies with his sisters. CheeLung had a keen sense of justice from his early years. He would harangue Grandmother about her gender discrimination and hotly refuse to benefit from it. In exasperation, she told the stubborn six-year-old, "You pollute my heart! I'm going to treat you like a girl since you take the side of the girls against me."

I knew it was not a personal thing that Grandmother disliked me. Whenever I was sick, I became a "patient" in her eyes and she stayed up nights checking my pulse, feeling my forehead for fever, brewing me herbal teas and barley water, wiping my face free of sweat. At such times, she could forget I was a girl. She should have been a nurse. Illness in anyone brought out the best side of her. I think she felt needed and useful at such times. But she had achieved that be-all and end-all of Chinese cultural ambition for a woman: she was a matriarch, with a son able to support her and a daughter-in-law to keep house for her. It would have meant a loss in social standing if she had gone to work. Occasionally, she did accept work (living in the empty apartment above the hardware shop to discourage robbers, helping cook for a relative's birthday or wedding celebration), but only when it was offered by a relative and she could label it as doing a favor for family.

She was at her most pleasant when she came home from doing one of those favors for a rich relative. She'd tell us stories about her younger days. How she locked her husband out of their bedroom when he stayed out late at night, and he would have to sleep in the hall without blanket or pillow. More often, she was bored and frustrated at having nothing to do, no gossip to share with a peer. Then she would spend her days lying on her bed, which was a wooden sofa with a coir-stuffed cushion, smoking and glaring at whichever girl-grandchild came in view. She was always physical in her temper tantrums. If her tea was not to her liking, she would slam her hand on the table, making the cup rattle. Or she'd throw her tea and cup at the wall. If she did not like the food at dinner, she threw her rice and bowl on the floor. Mother said it was because she was a child raised without a mother to teach her self-control and proper behavior. And that Father, raised by Grandmother, had had no chance to learn responsibility and restraint in his appetites either.

Grandmother was pleased when Brother LeeLang's friends came to the house. She'd rise from her bed-sofa and bring out drinks and fruit for them. When my friends came to visit, Grandmother lay on her bed-sofa and glared at them. She kept track of how many glasses of water they drank, how many pieces of fruit they ate, and complained about how greedy they were.

The year I was fourteen, Grandmother decided she would beat the laziness out of me. I wasted too much time reading, she said. She took to hiding any book I was reading as soon as I put it down. Luckily ours was a small house, a hall-cum-living room where Grandmother slept, the front bedroom which belonged to my parents, the back bedroom which the children shared, one bathroom, and the kitchen. I always found my book easily enough and thought of it as a game. This irritated her intensely and she began to find reasons to take a stick to me whenever Mother was out.

She did not use the rattan cane, Mother's chosen tool of punishment. Instead she would pull a stick from the firewood pile as long as her arm and twice its diameter. She was a tiny woman, four-feet-two, and weighed about 70 pounds. I was a hulking five-feet-four and crassly big for a Chinese girl. There was only one thing I could do—I ran away from her. Usually I could escape out the door and go to a friend's house until I knew Mother must have come home and it was safe to return. Grandmother never beat me when Mother was home because Mother said it was her (Mother's) job to discipline me.

I remember one afternoon I couldn't get to the door so I ducked into the bathroom and locked myself in. I stayed there all afternoon. Every time I peeked out, I saw Grandmother sitting with her stick across her knees, grimly determined to get me. It was stalemate for three hours. This was the last time she took a stick to me. I don't know if it was because Mother pointed out to her the difference in size between us and what the consequences could be if I had stayed and tried to defend myself. Or worse, if I forgot my respect for her age and hit her back.

Grandmother mellowed into a grumbling acceptance of me after I went to college and she positively approved of me when I graduated and began bringing money home. Before that happened, we had a final face-off which I remember vividly to this day.

It was my second year in college and I was home for the holidays. I had a government scholarship, which gave me financial independence. I was experiencing more freedom than I had ever known. The books I read in college, the ideas I could explore—I was drunk on Western ideas and mores. And more than ready to challenge authority.

I took my newly acquired pack of cigarettes and asked Grandmother if I could share her ashtray. She sniffed but did not say no. She eyed me with disapproval as I lit a cigarette and offered her one.

"Girls should not smoke," she said flatly as she took a Benson & Hedges and stuck it in her mouth.

I bent to light it for her. "But Grandmother, you smoke. And you're a girl, or you once were."

"I did not smoke until I was married to your grandfather," she said. "When you're married, you can do anything you like. But you're not married yet. No one will marry you if you smoke. A girl who smokes will do anything, even sleep with men."

Ouch! The problem with labels—there's enough truth in them to sting.

We had many smoking sessions after that, though she still grumbled that I should wait till I was married. Years later, after I was married and living in America, I dreamed of Grandmother. In the dream, I had found a baby elephant and was asking Mother if we could keep it. Grandmother was squatting under a rain tree, picking up the red seeds fallen around her. "Forget it; elephants cost too much to keep," she said, frowning disapprovingly at me. A week later, my brother LeeLang called to say Grandmother had died in her sleep.

Grandmother was not the only one in the family who tried to keep me eligible on the marriage market. LeeLang worried about my un-Chinese behavior and the tee-shirts and pants I wore most of the time. In my final year at college, he took me aside and offered me three hundred dollars to go buy a new wardrobe, pretty dresses. "The way you dress, going around like a hippie—how do you expect to attract a nice Chinese man like me?"

"Oh, Brother," I said, "I adore you, but I definitely do not want to attract a nice Chinese man like you."

5

The Odd-Job Man

Kett was a painter, a carpenter, an odd-job man. He was a young bachelor who built a small neat house at the edge of the jungle where our dirt lane ended in a sprinkling of forked footpaths and smelly ditches. We did not have sewers then. Everyone used out-houses and the excrement disposal man, who came every other day with his push cart, was a private entrepreneur paid by each household. Trash disposal was simple and on a do-it-yourself basis. We burned any trash that would burn and buried the rest. Not everyone was as conscientious as Mother. Some of our neighbors simply threw their trash out into the monsoon drain and the afternoon winds often brought the sour-mash smell of rotting vegetables into our house.

When Mother saw what a nice zinc roof Kett had put on his house, she asked him to replace our *attap*-thatch roof with zinc. Kett on the roof was a marvel to watch. He was so quick and sure in his movements as he took down sections of the *attap* thatch, carried the dry, rustling sheaves over to the vacant lot, and threw them into a big heap. He kept an eye on the sky as he worked. When the little cotton-ball clouds scudding across the sky like dragonflies on a pond disappeared and big grumpy thunderheads rumbled in, he would cover the hole in the roof with a tarpaulin so no rain ever fell into our house. Mother was so pleased, she kept saying what a good worker he was, what a pity he wasn't married, a nice man like Kett.

33

She introduced him to every nice girl she knew. She said such a nice man should not be wasted. His skills were always in demand and he made a good income, by our standards. When Kett got married, not to any of Mother's introductions, he invited us to his wedding. We were very happy for him and everyone blamed the bride when she ran away from him after two years. She had been a shy, aloof girl from Kuala Lumpur, an arranged match, and everyone agreed she must have disliked the poor neighborhood and our rough village life. Raised in a big town with flush toilets and streetlights, she couldn't take country life, they all said. Kett said she had been afraid of the jungle. A year later, he married again. This time, he married a local girl who became friends with everyone.

Kett's wife was a small woman with short permed hair. Her face was sadly marred by pockmarks. Apart from that, she was very pretty, with a ready smile and good teeth. She seemed to like wearing long-sleeved *samfu* tops, even on the hottest days. A few years later, she came by our house and told Mother she was leaving Kett. "Kett is so sweet and gentle in the day and always with other people. But he turns into a demon at night. He beats me whenever we mingle and join." She pulled up her sleeves and showed Mother the bruises on her arms. "They were black and yellow and green, the pitiful thing!" Mother told me, years later, when I was no longer a child in her eyes and she could tell me secrets with sexual content. It seemed that Kett had a distorted idea that sex was wicked and evil. He beat his wife for luring him into evil whenever he gave in to his sexual appetites. It was her fault for being wanton. A good wife would be a sexless companion and bear him a child immediately after the marriage was consummated, so he would not have to do the "evil" thing again. And again. Kett's wife cried, "It is my fault for being unable to conceive. If I had been able to get pregnant, we would be so happy together. I kept hoping each time he beat me, it would be the last time, that I would be pregnant. But my blood flows every moon and then it is to do, all over again." Kett was desperate for a child and had increased his attempts with attendant beatings the last year. Mrs. Kett had finally given up hope. "I can't bear it anymore—I hurt all the time. I'm going home to my mother. I've gotten employment at the shoe factory."

Kett went and begged her to come back many times. She never did. He never married again.

Before I learned her story from Mother, I asked Kett why his wife had left him. He shook his head and gazed at the dirt lane leading to Meru Road, the lane she had walked the last time, carrying a cloth bundle of her belongings. He shook his head sadly. "The jungle frightened her," he finally said and walked away, his shoulders drooping, his back bowed like a tired old man.

I thought poor Kett was terribly unlucky, to have married two women with the same silly fear. I was not afraid of the jungle, or only a teeny bit afraid. That was because of Mother. She never let me go in there, said bad things lurked there under the trees—tigers, baboons, poisonous snakes, maybe even bad men who'd rape a girl. I didn't know what "rape" actually meant, but I knew it was an unspeakable thing and worse than death to happen to a girl.

I remember the afternoon our zinc roof was finished. Kett told me and Brother we could come and help him fire the *attap* trash. This was long before his failed marriages, before frown-lines grew on his face, when life was still simple and Kett was a soft-spoken, fresh-faced young man, who was sure and clever with his hands and tools, who knew how to build a home. We followed him eagerly and were gratified when he allowed us to take the rolled newspapers he lit and to thrust them into the bottom of the huge *attap* pile. The dry thatch caught readily. Soon, a roaring bonfire spiraled dark oily smoke in a column into the sky. We were driven further and further back by the fierce heat. From a distance, the heated air shimmered like warped glass. Looking through its haze, our little house with its new roof seemed to ripple and shift. The front door moved; it became a dark hole that gaped with malice, with a hunger that needed and cried for human sacrifice. My eyes watered from the smoke. When I blinked them clear, our house was the firm, ordinary home we were used to, and seemed even pleasanter, with its roof-zinc sparkling sunlight back into the sky.

Kett stayed until the *attap* was all burned away and only a small smoldering heap of cinders remained. "That will make good fertilizer for fruit trees," he said, nodding his head at the blackened earth left by the bonfire. Then he packed his tools and strode whistling down the lane, toward the jungle's edge, to the neat little house he had built to hold his dreams of home and family.

6
Egg Noodles

The kitchen table was where we ate all our meals. It was where Mother made treats like egg noodles for birthdays. The long strings of noodles symbolized long life and Mother spent a whole afternoon kneading the dough, rolling them out, and cutting them by hand. We got wet and soapy scrubbing the flour out of the wood surface after she was done. That night, we'd feast on soup noodles and the birthday celebrant got the largest bowl of noodles to eat. Except when it was Grandmother's birthday.

Grandmother was not allowed to eat a big bowl of noodles even though she wanted to: she always threw up afterward, if she did. Then she would lie on her sofa moaning that she was dying. "Not an auspicious thing to do on a birthday!" Mother would say. Not allowing her the big bowl did not work either. Grandmother would throw a tantrum instead of vomiting. Rocking on her stool, she would curse Mother for being a hard, unfilial daughter-in-law: "Aiiyiee, I knew it the first time I saw your face—I knew you would be wicked and cruel to me; you have no respect for your husband's mother! Making me starve on my birthday. You're wishing for my death so you don't have to look after me anymore! Oh, what a miserable person I am, widowed in my youth and eating bitter sorrow in my old age!"

At this point, Father invariably went away. Like the Cheshire cat in *Alice's Adventures in Wonderland*, he never stayed around when there was trouble. We children would pat her bony arm awkwardly and tell her not to cry, that she could have more noodles tomorrow. She paid us no notice, aiming her lamentations at Mother and the thin plywood wall that divided us from our neighbors. The first few birthdays, the neighbors had come to inquire why the old lady was so upset. Later, they became accustomed to her keening on her birthday. We eventually did, too, and returned to eating our (by then) cold noodles. Even cold, the noodles were delicious. They were slippery and springy, hard to keep from slipping out of your mouth. I could sympathize with Grandmother wanting to eat lots of them.

Every night, we did our homework at the kitchen table. Homework was a ritual—you did it unless you were really sick and could prove it with a high fever, at which point Mother put you to bed and concocted various nasty, herbal remedies for you to drink. Her cures for colds and fevers invariably tasted foul and smelled strongly of raw onion and dead insects. None of us told Mother we felt sick if we could help it.

On rainy nights, Father would stay home and read a book while we did our homework. Apart from our schoolbooks, all the books in the house belonged to father. He was always buying fiction—Chinese paperback books with colorful covers—of handsome Chinese *kungfu* knights who could run a thousand *li* in a night without tiring, who could leap lightly and land silent as a leaf on roof tiles above villains plotting against the Empire. I looked through his shelves, hoping to find one with English that I could read. The one treasure I chanced upon in his collection, when I was in grade six, was a bilingual edition of Margaret Mitchell's *Gone with the Wind*. I remember the delight with which I read the book. Unfortunately for me, the rest of his collection consisted entirely of vertical rows of Chinese print that I could not read.

I made the mistake of wishing I could read Chinese to my father. "Blame your mother!" Father said, glaring at Mother. "I wanted you to go to Chinese schools. The stubborn woman insisted you should all go to the schools of the red-haired devils."

"All our rich relatives send their children to English schools. We're not in China anymore. There is only menial work for people who don't know English," Mother said grimly. "You should look at what your relatives do, not listen to what they say. Why, just the other day, your cousin was telling me the Methodist Girls' School was a better school than the Convent School and that I should enroll ChoyKam (that was my Chinese name) there."

"So, send ChoyKam to the Methodist Girls' School. They have nicer uniforms there," Father said.

"I'm sending her to the Convent. Your cousin's daughter is still going to the nuns. If they are not good, how come she hasn't transferred her daughter? I may be poor," Mother said scornfully, "but I'm not stupid. Like some people I could mention!"

At this point in their conversation (and many similar conversations), Father would remember he had something to do in town. He'd wheel his bicycle out the garden gate and speed down Meru Road into town, to where he had friends and the streets had lights.

The best fried noodle vendor in town had his stall in the alley by the corner coffee shop. When Mother had a whole dollar to spare after paying the bills for the seven household necessities (water, electricity, roof [rent], rice, oil, salt, and sugar), she would send me on my bike to the noodle stall. For a dollar, I would get five of the twenty-cent packets: a handful of thick yellow noodles, fried with bean sprouts and spiced with soy sauce and a dash of hot cayenne peppers. For thirty cents, you got an egg as well.

The noodle seller was a thin man whose ribs and chest hairs showed through the thin cotton of his singlet. He was a chain smoker, a lit cigarette always dangling from the mouth in his mournful face. For take-away customers, the noodle seller plopped the noodles onto newspapers each lined with a section of banana leaf and his boy would wrap and tie them up.

There was always a queue waiting for orders to be prepared. Often, the customers ahead of me would ask for the thirty-cent package. The noodle man would reach for an egg in the cardboard rack of eggs, crack it with his thumb, and break it into the huge wok, all this using only one hand. I tried it once at home and made a mess on the kitchen floor: when I pressed my thumb into my egg, it shattered and sent wet innards of egg everywhere.

It was fascinating to watch the egg cooking—to see its transparent albumen turn solid and white. Then the noodle man would swirl the yolk and white together with his steel spatula, stir-frying the noodles and egg together until little specks of white and gold on the noodles, like dandruff on golden hair, were the only evidence that an egg had been added to the mix.

Mother said the stall was at a good location—it had good *feng shui* (wind-water flow). Everyone who had held that spot had done a thriving business. As far as I could go back in memory, the fried noodle stall had been there. "What was there before?" I asked.

"It was a soup-noodle stall," Mother remembered. "The best noodle soup in town . . . until the War."

The soup-noodle vendor had been famous for his springy noodles and his delicious soup, Mother said. Even during the great World War, he had maintained the quality and tastiness of his soup, to the wonder of the townspeople. All knew meat was hard to come by in those days, when the Japanese troops took all the pigs and chickens for themselves, and everyone was making do with boiled roots and cabbage water. How did he manage to get meat? or bones?—his soup tasted meaty. They shook their heads and suspected him of collaborating with the enemy. And every day, they stood in line at his stall to eat his soup noodles.

Until one day, the soup-noodle vendor was careless. A customer found a rat's tail in her soup. "It's a wonder the whole town didn't die of the plague. I never bought from him—he was too expensive. But your father used to eat there."

"What happened to the noodle man?" I asked.

"He disappeared," Mother said. "That low-life probably moved to another town where people didn't know about him and fed them rat soup."

7

Nursery Rhymes
& Proverbs Cantonese

In my home, we spoke Cantonese, a dialect of GuangDong Province in Southern China. I had a year's education in a Chinese kinder- garten and can write my name in Chinese. Though I can speak Cantonese, I am illiterate in written Chinese, and cannot speak Pei Hwa, the official language of the Chinese. Yet my mother tongue built the foundations for the writer I became.

My mother raised us on Cantonese nursery rhymes. The Chinese are indulgent with babies and will spend hours walking and rocking and crooning lullabies to lull a baby to sleep in their arms. When a child reaches the age of four, the showering of atten- tion and affections stops; all cuddling ceases. Non-babies are expect- ed to learn proper behavior and respect for their grown-ups. Proper Chinese do not show affection. Demonstrativeness is undignified. I did not hug or kiss my parents after toddlerhood until I was thirty- five and had been corrupted by American ways. I learned nursery rhymes from my mother to chant to my baby sisters who were 9 and 11 years younger than I. Since it rained almost every afternoon, I liked to sing the "Rain Song" to the babies.

Rain Song

Lokh yi mey
Sui jum kai
KoKo thum chai
sheong kai mai.
Shai lo jiok far hai
Far hai far kiork tai
Kum ho far hai
Yai lok lai.

Small drops are falling
Flooding the street.
Elder brother carries firewood
Up the street to sell.
Little brother wears embroidered shoes.
Elegant shoes on elegant feet,
Such fine shoes to step in mud.

Many were just nonsense rhymes but they had rhythm, assonance, rhyme, and tactile images. My favorite nonsense rhymes were "Round and Round" and "Moon Song."

Round and Round

Thum thum jeun, jeun far yeun.
Chow mye pang, lor mye teun.
Ah Ma kew ngo tai loong sheun.
Ngo m'tai, tai kai chai,
Kai chai tai, lor hui mai.
Mai chor kay tor lui? Saam pak ngan.
Kam yew tai, ngan yew tai,
Chiang Ah PoPo chut ley pai
Pai tak tor, mo loy hor.
Sam cheng siew jhow, leong twe ngor.
Ngor thow, ngorr may soong bey Ah Dhai Kum Por.
Kum Por m'jior oak, soong bey Ah Saam Soak.
Saam Soak kare pak ma, low shee lai dhong kwa.

Round and round the garden patch,
Fried rice cakes, sticky rice dough.
Mother calls me to see dragon boats.
I will not, I'm raising chickens.
Chickens are full-grown, off to market.
How much did I sell them for?
I sold them for three hundred taels.
I've got girdles of silver, girdles of gold,
I brought Old Grandma out to pray.
But it's not good to pray too much.
Three jars of spiced wine, a pair of geese,
I'll give their heads and tails to Grand-Aunt One.
Grand-Aunt One is not at home, send them to Uncle Three.
Uncle Three is out riding a white horse.
I'm a mouse dragging a winter melon!

"Moon Song" is another nonsense rhyme and quite racist at the
end, reflecting the Chinese xenophobia of earlier times.

Moon Song

Yuit kong kong, jhew dhey dhong
Leen sam mahn, jak ping long
Ping long heong, jak ji kheong
Ji kheong lart, my fu sart
Fu sart fu, my jwee dhu
Jwee dhu fey, my ngow pey
Ngow pey pork, my leng kork
Leng kork jeem, my ma peen
Ma peen cheong, hei oak leong
Oak leong ko, my jeong to
Tho chit choi, my lor koi
Lor koi yueen, my jhat sueen
Sueen jhum dhai, jhum sey k'farn kwei jai.

Moon so bright, shining on the earth's heart.
New Year's Eve, we pick nutmeg.
Nutmeg's fragrant, we pick ginger-root.

Ginger-root is hot, we buy mustard.
Mustard is bitter, we buy pig's stomach.
Pig's stomach is fatty, we buy leather.
Leather is thin, we buy ling nuts.
Ling nuts are sharp, we buy a horse whip.
Horse whip is long, we raise the roof beam.
Roof beam is high, we buy a knife.
Knife chops cabbage, we buy a basket.
Basket is round, we buy a boat.
Boat goes down, foreign devils drown.

Marriage was a hoped-for destiny for every child, regardless of sex. My mother sang this lullaby to the baby boys as well as to girls.

Lullaby

Oy ku kwai, oy ku kwai kwai tai kau meen
Lek ley jeong far dhai. Oy oy ku kwai.

Lullaby, lullaby my baby. Be good and sleep well.
Sleep and grow up to wear the wedding girdle. Lullaby.

Besides nursery rhymes, my mother was very fond of proverbs. She had a natural flair for telling stories and used proverbs as cleverly as a master chef uses spices. I often think that Cantonese proverbs are like bouillon cubes: they are always compact, evocative word pictures that pack a lot of meaning and punch. For instance, my mother would describe a friend who was boasting thus: "*Sek jho sween dhoq.* He has eaten garlic." Of another fretting over imaginary fears, she'd say: "*Wong dhei par dhong!* The Emperor fears cold!"

Growing up as I did, with a language that was terse, concentrated, and full of rhymes and images, it was natural for me to think in metaphors and to turn to the reading and writing of poetry. My mother's favorite teaching proverb was this: "*Wai yan wai dho dhay, soong fatt soong dho sai.* Helping others, do your very best. Sending Buddha, escort him to the West." She insisted we should do any task we accepted responsibly and completely. She did not believe in feeling sorry for oneself or in crying over bad luck: "*Mah sei, lok deih haahng.* The horse being dead, get down and walk." She said that

Myself at age 6 with boarder, Mr. Hung,
in front of the house still with an attap-thatch *roof*

Myself at age 14 with Mother and baby sisters ChoyNgor and ChoyChoy in the lane, Kelang (Boys) High School in the background

Myself at age 7 with Mother and brother CheeLung in the lane

since we were too poor to have horses, or a car, well then, we could walk, we were lucky, we had two good legs. But she was wrong about our having no horses; she gave us strong horses named "Integrity," "Brave Heart," and "Taking Responsibility"; she gave us steady horses named "Clean as Water, Never Sticky with Debts," "Good Will," and "Wearing Eyes to See People"; she gave us mountain-climbing horses named "Motivation" and "Respectfully Refusing to Quit." Endowed with such horses, I have never felt poor.

8

India Next Door

The neighbor's baby was screaming at three o'clock again. Ever since his mother brought him home from the hospital, we had heard his high-pitched wailing each afternoon like a faithful alarm clock. The Subramaniam family was of South Indian descent and they spoke Tamil at home. Like our household, the father and the children spoke English while the older womenfolk spoke their native tongue and used bazaar Malay to communicate with others. The rest of the neighbors were Chinese, like us, but they spoke different dialects. Most spoke Hokkien, as their ancestors came from the province of Fukien; one family spoke TeoChew, one Hainanese; and we spoke Cantonese.

Our Indian neighbors had dark skin, big eyes, thick black hair, very white teeth, high cheeks, and enviable high noses. Being Chinese, we had thin hair, flattened noses, and no cheekbones to speak of. We admired their profiles and tried to discover the secrets of their difference. Mother learned they brushed their teeth with charcoal and she tried it on us. We hated the taste and the gritty feel of left-behind ash.

The men in the Subramaniam family wore Western clothes, white shirts, ties, and black pants. The women were very traditional in all ways; they wore the form-fitting *choli* top, a petticoat, and a diaphanous over-dress called a *sari*, which is very graceful and doesn't need sewing. The *sari* is a six-yard length of forty-five-inch-wide gauzy material, plain pale colors or white, with a color stripe along the edge for everyday wear, dyed in rich strong colors and elaborately printed and threaded with gold and silver threads for special occasions. Sometimes, when I was playing in their house, Mrs. Subramaniam, whom we called "Tangachii," meaning "Aunt" in Tamil, would let me watch as she put on her "going out" *sari*. I sat entranced as she gathered a yard of the cloth into pleats, held it against her belly button with her left hand, and spun herself slowly, smoothly into the rest of the long cloth that her right hand held out at her side. She stopped turning when she had about a yard and a half of cloth left in her right hand. Pleating the remnant, she tossed the loose end over her left shoulder to hang in a drape over her back. I never knew how she made the *sari* stay up. It was like a magic show. I think it pleased Mrs. Subramaniam to impress me. She had tried to teach me, one long afternoon, to put on a *sari*, and finally told me to stick to *samfu*, Chinese tunic and pants. Tangachii wore a lot of jewelry. All twenty-four-karat gold. Gold chains, bangles, bracelets, earrings, nose-rings, toe-rings. She always had twenty gold bangles on her wrists. It was her dowry, her fortune, she said. It was also her bank. Every time she saved enough money from her housekeeping allowance, she bought a piece of good gold to wear.

Mrs. Subramaniam's mother-in-law lived with them, like our grandmother lived with us. Old Mrs. S. had salt-and-pepper hair she wore in a bun at the back of her neck. She always wore plain white *cholis* and *saris*. Her nice *saris* had silver stripes; her everyday ones had brown or dark blue borders. I often wondered how she managed to keep her clothes clean as she had a terrible habit of chewing betel nuts mixed with lime, not the fruit, but the powdered lime- stone that was used for fertilizer. Her favorite pastime was to sit by the front door with her betel-nut tray, fold a betel nut in a fresh, green betel leaf, dab a bit of white lime on it, and chew slowly and blissfully for ten minutes or more. Then she would hawk and shoot out a stream of bright red spittle into the road before the house. None of it ever dripped on her clothes!

There is a Javanese song about a Malay warrior-hero of legend, Hang Tuah: How he visited Majapahit and all the women swooned over him and had to console themselves. "Here is betel leaf. Take it to allay the pangs of a whole day's love—but you will still yearn for him." The practice of betel-nut/leaf chewing is dying out; it was common among the lower-caste and older Indians and shunned by their children, even then.

The Subramaniams were Hindu Indians and had many gods, like our household. They had framed pictures of their gods on their walls. One thing I remember about their gods is that they were extremely over-worked—they all had multiple arms to keep up with the many things they had to do. Ganesh, the elephant-headed god, was my favorite—his picture showed a benign gray elephant face with elephant ears, amused eyes, and a long gray trunk on a gray human potbellied body with four arms, riding a big rat.

This was the story Mrs. Subramaniam told me: Ganesh was the son of the gods Shiva and Parvati. His mother, Parvati, had told the six-year-old Ganesh to guard the door while she took a bath. Shiva, returning home unaware that he had a son, was angered by the young boy who refused to allow him into his house, so, in a godlike rage, he cut off Ganesh's head. Emerging from her bath, Parvati was most displeased to find she had regained a husband and lost a son. She told Shiva to restore his son's life. It had been a long bath. Ganesh's brain had died. Shiva dashed out and grabbed the head of the first creature he met and revived Ganesh with an elephant's head. Which might explain why Ganesh is the kindest of the Hindu gods.

All the god-pictures were festooned with garlands of fresh jasmine and frangipani flowers. The Subramaniam house was pleasantly perfumed with their flowery smells, a light layering over the heavier persistence of coriander and cumin.

I think the cumin smell came from the curry spices they kept. I knew the coriander smell came from the seeds that old Mrs. S. chewed when she was not chewing betel nut and having a spitting contest with herself. The family ate curried dishes with every meal: curried fish, curried *dahl* beans, curried chicken, mutton, and peas and other vegetables they cooked and mashed up into brown sauces to eat with *bismahti* (brown unhusked) rice. They saved their plates and forks for when they had company (very rare) and used disposable sections of banana leaf and their hands for regular meals.

Our families had very different dinner routines. Our father came home at five and we all ate together, bowls of white rice and stir-fried vegetables with occasional slivers of pork or chicken using chopsticks to shovel the food into our mouths. Then he went out for the evening and we children did our homework while Mother sewed or chatted with Grandmother. Grandmother did not chew betel nut; she smoked her own hand-rolled cigarettes and threw the butts into the inch of water in the enamel-ware spittoon by her bed-sofa. Our Indian neighbors ate their dinner in shifts four hours behind us. First Mr. Subramaniam and the sons were served dinner on banana leaf sections by the women. The women and daughters ate only after the males had finished, just like they had to walk a few feet behind the men when they went out together. They all ate with their right hands, rolling their rice and curry into a bite-sized ball and popping it into their mouths. Mother said it was forbidden to eat with the left hand because that was the hand one used for wiping in the bathroom.

Mother asked Mrs. Subramaniam how Indians got their wonderfully high noses. Mrs. S. invited her to come and watch old Mrs. S. at three o'clock. I went too as I was curious. When we walked in, old Mrs. S. was giving the new baby a bath. *"Baik-lah, lu mari, tengok ini.* Good, you come and watch this," she said in Malay. She shoved her right thumb up the mouth of the baby and hoisted him off her knees with just that point of contact. Then she lowered him to rest on her knees again. At this point, the baby broke out with the wail we had heard every afternoon for the last month. *"Lu mesti buat itu taip-tiap hari kapada anak dari mingu beranak sampai tiga bulan lepas.* You must do this every day from first week of birth until three months old," old Mrs. Subramaniam said as she calmly soaped and rinsed the baby, as if it were not screaming at all. *"Terima kaseh, banyak terima kaseh!* Love received, much love received!" Mother thanked her and we rushed back to our house while we could still pretend we had not been shocked senseless. "This is as terrible as foot-binding," Mother finally said when we were in our house. "Your future brothers' and sister's noses will just have to stay the way they come."

9
Chickens

One afternoon, I came home from school to find Mother sitting in the dark in our bedroom with a burning candle and a basket of eggs. "What are you doing?" I asked. She said she was "candling eggs" to pick out the fertilized eggs for hatching. She held each egg before the candle flame and showed me what to look for: the tiny shadow-dot which meant it was fertile. I knew about sex among the chickens. I had often seen our neighbor's rooster pounce on an unwary hen and bite its comb while it shrieked and got away as soon as it could.

We started our chicken farming with a broody hen Mother bought from a friend. And twenty fertilized eggs from the "candling." Mother nestled the eggs in a box of straw and the brown broody hen sat on them immediately. Mother got angry with Brother and me because we kept trying to peek under the broody hen for chicks. It seemed forever (it took 20 days) before we finally heard a peep-peep and all at once, from under the speckled brown breast of the broody hen, two bright eyes in a yellow, fuzzy head were looking up at us. The broody hen looked pleased and proud as only a silly hen could look. But we told her she was wonderful and praised her so she would let us play with her chick.

Each time the mother hen left its box to peck at its food and water bowls, Brother and I crouched eagerly over the exposed eggs, hoping an egg would hatch. Several eggs had cracks in their shells. Then one egg moved. It wobbled. Its cracks widened. It split open. A wet, dark, bedraggled bony thing, with a too-large head, tottered from the shell halves. It cheeped. And cheeped. We stared at it, fascinated. It was alive! I was surprised at how ugly it was. The mother hen rushed back and plunked her soft warm body over it. Later, when we saw it again, its down had dried the color of sunshine and it was a roly-poly fur-ball, just like its sister. We took turns holding it in our cupped palms. I did not care much for poultry; the hens and roosters always wore an air of self-consequence as they stepped around the yard, squawking loudly whenever they found a bit of dirt to eat. But I loved the baby chicks. I thought it was too bad they had to grow into self-important hens with sharp beaks.

The miracle of chickens hatching was repeated many times in our house. Mother built a large henhouse under the guava tree out back and we raised many chickens, mainly for their eggs. Brother and I took turns delivering eggs each week to the bigger houses on Meru Road.

When the layers stopped producing eggs, we had chicken for dinner. Mother made me watch her slaughter them because she said I should learn the skill for when I had to keep house for my husband. She gripped the hen by its legs firmly with her left hand, pulled its throat back into that same hand, plucked a spot bare of neck feathers and slit its throat with a sharp knife. All this was done so fast, I never could follow all her motions. Then she held the chicken upside down to let its blood drain into a bowl of salt water. This she steamed into blood pudding later for Grandmother Tham whose favorite late-night snack was blood pudding. And bishop's noses, pig's brains, pig's lung soup, and fish-heads, everything I was glad I didn't have to eat.

After the chicken stopped bleeding, Mother flipped the chicken's head over its back and around its wings. Then she left it on the kitchen floor. The chicken was not dead at this point. It fluttered its wings and threw itself around, flopping all over the kitchen floor. Meanwhile, mother calmly filled a large pot with water and lit the wood stove. When the water was boiling, the chicken had stopped moving. Mother held it by the legs and parboiled it in the pot. Then she plucked its feathers in a basin of cold water. I knew that not everyone slaughtered their own chickens. The chicken man at the market would kill and clean a chicken for you for a few cents extra. I resolved to study hard, earn a lot of money, and never have to slaughter my own chickens.

Mother said she had learned the proper way to slaughter chickens by the time she was ten. She shook her head over my slowness in learning. Each time a layer was declared "ready for the knife," she'd ask me if I would like to try my hand. I said I would rather watch her do it.

"Each subsequent generation grows softer and less able to deal with natural things," Mother said as she saw my daughters politely refuse to eat chicken she had curried because it had broken bones in it. "Your father's mother was a farm girl. *She* used to slaughter pigs and monkeys."

Strange Things

I have eaten pig's blood
pudding. Also *chee zee*, "pig's dung"
as we called golden cheddar,
the white man's delight.

Once I ate baby swallows, canned
before they knew feathers. Snake
have I eaten; and frog in my youth
when meat was scarce at our table.
We rarely ate chicken; Mother kept
hens to sell their eggs.

Rainy days meant a good night for frogs
in the grass of Chattiah's field
when the cowherd's boy had gone home
with his two cows. Once, I saw him
topping off a milk bottle with water
from the gutter.

A bottle for Mr. Wong,
the schoolmaster who ate chicken
and chocolates and cheese,
who was proud to be pale
like an Englishman, who drank
fresh milk heated every night.
Once, he squeezed my pre-teen breasts

when his wife was out, saying
things I did not understand
as I dropped her eggs and ran.
He had a voice like the best butter
left out overlong, slightly rancid.

—from *Tigerbone Wine*

10

Leila's Wedding

Mr. and Mrs. Subramaniam were our next-door neighbors. "Tangachii" (Tamil for "Aunt"), or "Achii" for short, was Mr. Subramaniam's second wife, and she was pregnant most of the time. With them lived their six children and Mr. S.'s mother. Mr. S. also had a daughter, Leila, and a son, Chandran, by his dead first wife. I admired Leila—she was five years older than I, and very beautiful to my eyes.

Leila had milky chocolate skin unlike my sallow yellow. I had slanty eyes; she had big round orbs. I had short, thin, dull hair. Her hair was what I imagined the fairy-tale Rapunzel's hair must have been like. When she unbraided it, her hair hung down to the backs of her knees. Once a month, Leila rubbed coconut oil vigorously into her hair. She would sit in the scorching afternoon sun for half an hour, "for the oil to cook and make the hair shine," she said. Waiting, she busied her hands going through her hair with a close-toothed comb, checking for lice. I wanted to try the coconut oil, but Mother said, "Waste of good oil and your hair will smell like Indian hair. Be content with what you're given. Though the crow bathes three times a day, he will still not have white feathers."

When Leila was fifteen, the thirty-three-year-old brother of her dead mother sent a matchmaker to ask for her hand. When Mrs. Subramaniam invited us to the wedding, she told mother that marriage with close kin was a custom of southern Indians.

I was shocked a little by how young a bride Leila would be. I knew my own mother had been married to my father at age fourteen, but that was due to the war. In 1956, Chinese girls were not married until they had at least finished high school. I was relieved when Mother assured me she wanted me to go to college and to have a job before marrying.

I asked Leila if she liked getting married. She shrugged and rolled her eyes. "I don't know. I've only seen my uncle a few times. I like the shopping, for *saris* and linen, especially jewelry. It feels funny having to call my grandmother 'Mother-in-law' after the wedding. At least I know she won't be mean to me."

After that conversation, Leila was kept too busy to talk to me. Preparations for the wedding occupied the Subramaniams and more and more people, Indian friends and relatives, came to help. The house next door became like a reverse clown-car I saw one time at the visiting circus. People kept going into the house to help with advice, food preparation, and decoration, to provide proper admiration for the dowry of colorful *saris,* the electric fan, the radio with AM and short-wave bands (FM was the frequency used by the police and banned for ordinary radios), the gleaming brass pots for the new bride to cook with, even the certificate of sale for a refrigerator. A very small one, true, but it was a refrigerator. A grand gift indeed. No one in our lane had a refrigerator. The bill of sale was framed and placed prominently on the dowry table. It certified in English that Mr. Subramaniam had purchased a such-and-such refrigerator to be delivered to the couple after the wedding on the hire-purchase plan.

Mother said Mr. Subramaniam was giving Leila "very large face" (prestige) by spending so much on her wedding. I was aware how important "face" was, and is, to the Chinese. I had noticed there were two ways my parents' associates increased "face." The first method was by outright boasting: telling everyone, even indifferent strangers, how rich you were, whether in wealth you'd gotten yourself or via progeny, how many successful and filial (meaning they gave you money) children you had, how extravagant you had been or could be in the foods you ate, the expensive hospitals where you had gone for treatment, how your sickness was much worse than theirs, etc. We called such face-grabbers "garlic-breaths." The other method was even more negative—you told your host his fish was not as fresh as fish you had eaten at the Shangri-La restaurant in

Hong Kong, thereby letting him and all present know you were an epicure and much-traveled man of the world.

Later, I was to realize that other cultures had their own ways of achieving status. Men of the Mediterranean and South American cultures told entertaining tales of scrapes they got into chasing and getting women, a subtle way of bragging about their libidos. I wish the Chinese face-grabbers had a fraction of their creativity and style. Their way of gathering status did not diminish others.

Mr. Subramaniam rented chairs and tables and a huge tent-top tarpaulin. Workmen came and built a temporary scaffolding for the tarp. They built a platform with a canopied throne on it—a wooden bench with a high back to which they stapled red velvet trimmed with gold braid. On the morning of the wedding, a Sunday, the girls of the family and friends strung fresh flowers with needle and thread. They decorated the throne and its canopy and the sides of the platform with orange and gold marigolds, white jasmine, and gold-centered white frangipani. I especially liked the strands of marigolds that hung from the canopy to make a golden fringe. Special large garlands of white flowers strung with red and gold beads were delivered by the florist for the bride and groom to wear.

All day long, guests and relatives arrived, the men in Western dress of white shirt and tie and black pants, the women in *saris* as bright as tail feathers on peacocks. I loved the clothes the women wore. Each had a *choli*, a form-hugging top made of satin in a solid color to match one of the colors in her *sari*. The *choli* had tight sleeves that ended above the elbow; it had a low-cut scoop neckline and it ended at various levels below the breasts. The bare midriff that the draped *sari* did not completely cover was the beauty spot for Indians. Mrs. Subramaniam never bought or made pregnancy clothes, unlike my mother. She just wound her sari fewer times around her expanding waist. I remember thinking, at the time, that the Indian *sari* was much kinder to middle-aged female bodies than the Chinese *cheongsam*, a form-fitting sheath-dress with its choking collar. It had side-slits to tantalize with glimpses of thigh instead of midriff.

At four o'clock, the time set for the wedding, a shining black Renault sedan bumped its way down our dirt lane. The guests started chanting in Tamil: "The groom is here! Bring out the bride!" Chandran, Leila's brother, translated for me. Like everybody there, I stood and watched the groom, a middle-aged Indian man in a dark

Western suit, as he sat in the rear of the car, pretending not to know
we were all staring at him. It was a typical Malaysian day, humid
and hot, about 95 degrees Fahrenheit. I could see the groom's face
through the open car window, the sweat beading and rolling in dis-
tinct drops down his forehead. He had soaked two large white handkerchiefs, mopping his face, before Leila was led out of the house by
a flurry of *saried* aunts. They escorted her to the throne with much
fussing and straightening of her hair and *sari* and seated her there.
Then they got the groom out of the car, hung garlands on him, and
seated him beside her.

I was used to seeing Leila in everyday clothes: loose blouse
with calf-length skirt or her old school pinafore. The Subramaniams
had stopped sending her to school after she was thirteen, considering her education adequate for a woman at that point. This was the
first time I had actually seen her in a *sari* and *choli*, though her stepmother and grandmother wore *saris* all the time. Chandran said she
would have to wear a *sari* all the time now that she was married.
Skirts were considered clothes for children or servant-girls.

The bridal *sari* Leila wore was a heavy silk of bougainvillea
pink, with painted flowers and paisley, with gold thread all over.
She seemed taller and slimmer. She seemed almost a stranger, with
her hair braids coiled and piled high on her head, ornamented with
little white flowers and glittering jewelled pins. Leila's eyes seemed
huge and startled, outlined in *kohl*. She had a pink tear-shaped beauty dot painted in the middle of her forehead. The strangest new
thing about her was the nose ring. She had not had a pierced nose
the last time I saw her. Her nose ring was an enormous gold hoop. It
hung from her right nostril down to her lips. It reminded me of the
nose rings cows and water buffalo had to wear so the herd-boy
could easily control them.

A little bald-headed Indian priest wearing a white loincloth
and garlands of flowers was busy on the platform. He had a fire
going in a brass pan and was chanting prayers over it. "That's the
sacred fire," Chandran told me, proud to show off his knowledge.
The priest chanted over the fire a long time. Occasionally, he made
mystic passes with his hands over it; then he waved a bowl of water,
a coconut, and an incense burner over the fire, chanting all the
while. Next he repeated his prayers and gestures over the bent
heads of the bride and groom while they sat and watched their nails

grow on their fingers. Then he resumed chanting over the sacred fire
while the crowd of guests chatted and mostly ignored him. An hour
later, when I had gone home, bathed, and returned, he was still
praying. "Did he do anything while I was gone?" I whispered to
Chandran, who rolled his eyes as he replied. "Nah, just droned on
and on, same as now."

Finally, the priest finished chanting his prayers, and the chief
aunt, who Chandran said was his mother's eldest married sister (she
was actually the second sister but the first was not wed and unmarried sisters didn't count), led the groom and bride in a clockwise circle around the sacred fire. They circled it seven times. "Each circle is
a prayer for the gods to bless them with food, strength, happiness,
wealth, children, cows, and love," Chandran said. Chandran was
eleven then, a year older than I. He was always friendly to me and
never scornful of girls' company, as were my brother and the other
neighborhood boys. I liked him until the year I was fourteen, when
he showed me a letter, purportedly from a French girl, a pen pal,
that described a sexual encounter in such graphic detail that my face
felt hot while reading it. I decided he was growing up too fast for me
and avoided him thereafter.

"Good, they're married. Now we eat!" Chandran pulled me
over to the buffet tables where all the food had been laid out, pro-
tected by banana leaves from uninvited flies just as the invited
guests surged up from their chairs and headed for the food.

Leila and her uncle/husband sat on the throne for hours during the feast. The chief aunt brought them a plate of food and they
shyly fed each other a few bites. Then they sat on display and
received the good wishes and presents of the long line of guests. The
guests clasped the couple's hands briefly and then touched their
own heads and hearts. To show sincerity, I guessed. I didn't want to
ask Chandran; he'd take it as another opportunity to feel superior to
me.

I enjoyed the wedding feast. I loved Indian curries and goodies, especially the sweet *gulap*, powdered milk balls, fried and then
soaked in sugar syrup. When I was tired, I went home. Later, in bed,
I could hear the wedding band playing their sitars and drums. I
could not decide if I liked Indian music. It seemed to me Indian
music was like putting your ear to the chest of a person with twenty
hearts all beating and thrumming away in different rhythms until

your own heart was pulled into their wild jungle beat, filling your head with hints of uncomfortable mysteries, strange yearnings, empty places in the heart.

I thought of Leila and felt sorry for her and her uncle/husband: having to sit stiffly and long on display. I remembered I had attended part of a Malay wedding, which normally lasted three days. Their *Bersanding* (sitting-in-state) ceremony was even more elaborate than Leila's. I had been younger then and recalled eating delicious beef *rendang* (beef cubes cooked with cayenne and coconut milk until dry) and being given hard-boiled eggs to take home. It had not occurred to me to think of the bridal couple's feelings then. I resolved I would not have an elaborate traditional wedding when I grew up and got married.

Luckily for me, Chinese weddings were more Westernized. The old tradition of the bride, in red brocade jacket and long, black silk skirt, face hidden under an elaborate headdress and red silk scarf, being conveyed in a sedan chair carried by two bearers and preceded by gongs and cymbals, was past. Modern Chinese brides wore the Western white lace and tulle or organdy. My parents' wedding photograph shows him in Western suit and her in a white bridal gown, holding a sheaf of gladiolas. Mother told me she had been married in a traditional Chinese red and black brocade, a tunic and long skirt, but that they had dressed up in the photo studio's wardrobe for the picture. She said the first Western gowns that Chinese brides wore had been pink. There had been strong resistance among the elders to bridal white, white being the Chinese color for mourning. They thought white at a wedding meant bad joss, bad luck. The first bride to wear white in our family was Grand-Aunt Two. All the elders were convinced there would be a death in the family or a loss in the business. But nothing bad occurred that year, try as they did to link a misfortune to the white dress.

At the Chinese weddings of relatives I attended, I thought the main event was the wedding banquet, where the bridal couple visited each table of feasting guests to toast them with imported French brandy, Hennessy or Remy Martin. Weak drinkers diluted their brandy with ginger ale. The bride, being a woman and weak, was allowed to switch to Chinese tea for her toasts while the guests did their best to get the groom drunk for his wedding night. Then the guests went around challenging others to *"Yum Sing!* Drink the cup empty!" Wedding banquets had to be extravagant: the greater the cost, the more "face" the groom's parents gained. Some families got such "large faces" that their stomachs went shrunken for months after. But they did not mind; they had flaunted their success as parents—they had raised their son to true Chinese adulthood. I knew that one was not considered "adult" until married. Parents of unmarried middle-aged people were viewed as failed parents.

The actual rite of a Chinese wedding, the tea ceremony, had been simplified. Where bride and groom used to wear ancient Ching Dynasty costumes and held both ends of the marriage knot, a red sash with a large, intricate knot in its middle, and knelt on cushions to *kowtow* (knocking their foreheads on the floor) three times before offering cups of tea to parents and gods and ancestors, modern couples wore Western dress and bowed from the waist. One custom had survived, the practice of hiring an *Ah Por*, Old Grandma, to direct the tea ceremony. She told the bridal couple when to bow, who to bow to, and so on. She announced the wedding to the ancestors. She always shouted this out very loudly, in case the ancestors had wandered off from their altar, I suppose. Or maybe, being dead, they did not hear too well any more.

Later, the Subramaniam family moved to a bigger house on the other side of town and we lost touch with them. Whether Leila was happy in her marriage was not a question I could ask my mother, or Leila's family. Love and happiness were White Men notions. Only movie stars and emperors demanded love. Ordinary Chinese did not. *"Wo chung-yi ni"* (I like you) and *"Wo si-fun ni"* (You please me) were the most passionate declarations of love permitted a respectable woman. *"Wo shet ni"* (I have affection for you) was reserved for expressions of parental and filial love. *"Wo ai ni"* (I want/love you!) was for adulteresses, loose women, concubines, too wanton and too lustful for good women, proper wives, to use. *Ai ching* was the term for love between man and woman, the *ai* meaning love, erotic, the *ching* meaning love, kindred/affinity. The characters, reversed and used in formal salutations in letters, meant "Beloved Kindred" in that context, and the *Ai* became respectable for ordinary usage. The ordinary woman was content if her husband treated her well, that is, gave her a house to keep, children to raise. If he also came home every night and did not beat her, she had to be happy. "Happy" was the broad word we had for all good feelings. When I learned the many gradations, the spectrum of words the

English language had for happy emotions: "joy," "gladness," "merri-
ment," "serenity," "delight," "felicity," "ecstasy," "rapture," "bliss,"
I tried to find the Chinese equivalents for them. I found none. I
found the highest level of Chinese happiness was to have a "large
face and a filled belly."

I guessed Leila was happy as we heard no rumors of beatings.
Years and years later, we did hear that a grown-up Chandran had
beaten his stepmother for adultery with the math tutor of her small
children. Mr. Subramaniam died a few years later. He never found
out about the affair, never knew he had lost "face."

Secrets

1

Old Pui, our neighbor, haunted backlanes
on his bicycle to collect juicy news
for himself, table-scraps for his pig.
He'd tell Mother bits of gossip as he fed his pig,
smiling as it gulped down all he brought.
The pig lived behind his house, hidden
from passers-by and government men.

The apple of Old Pui's eye
was his firstborn son,
an all-A's student, who told my brother
he never studied, and lured him out to play.
One night, Mother saw the light
in a hole in the wall, woke Brother
to show him the effortless student
up all night over his books.

Just before New Year, men would come
with a truck and poles, truss up the
squealing hairy pig. They'd weigh it
suspended from a pole braced
by two muscular men.
After five years, five pigs, someone
told the law. Old Pui quit

animal husbandry, took up
match-making instead.
Shaking his head, he said,
"Pigs are more profitable."

2

The Yap family next door had seven sons
who sold vegetables at the market, two
daughters, five daughters-in-law and
fifteen miscellaneous grandchildren.
All the very young had animal names
to evade the notice
of malicious ghosts or gods.
Three-year-old Tae Kiah, Little Pig,
played bare-bottomed in the lane
though his mother diapered him constantly.
Grandmother Yap shook her head.
"Takes after his Fifth Uncle," she sighed.

When her fifth son came home on visits
from Tanjong Rambutan Asylum,
they closed their doors and windows.
The one time we saw Fifth Uncle,
he was running up the lane, naked
as a newborn until his brothers
caught him and dragged him back
into the protection of clothes,
love and locked doors.

11

Hot Water

A new movie came to town, a movie titled *Miss ChoyChoy.*
Neighbors told mother the Regal Theater was running a promotion
campaign that offered a grand prize of one hundred dollars (my
father earned that much in a whole month) for any girl or woman
who had that name and could provide documented proof. My ten-
month-old baby sister was named ChoyChoy. All excited, Mother
got out the birth certificate which had her name in English and
Chinese, the exact same characters as the movie heroine's name. She
fed us lunch, dressed up the baby, and set off on the two-mile walk
to the movie theater. She left Brother LeeLang, aged fourteen, and
me, aged twelve, in charge of the two younger kids.

It was Sunday. Father was out as usual. We had done our
schoolwork. We had taken the little ones into the wild grass across
the ditch and hunted leaf spiders. We had held fighting matches
until our captive spiders tucked their legs under their shiny-black
rotund abdomens and refused to move. When it began to rain, we
returned indoors and played pirates raiding their ship (an up-ended
table). When my three-year-old sister ChoyNgor settled down for
her nap, I decided to wash my hair. I heated water in a large
saucepan for the bath. Our stove was a waist-high table with cement
firebowls in which we cooked with wood fires. I do not remember
what happened but as I was lifting the pot of boiling water, it
slipped from my hands and liquid pain cascaded down my front. I

must have screamed, for my brothers came running to the kitchen. Five-year-old CheeLung reacted most resourcefully. He grabbed the large plastic dipper on the water jar and flung cold water over my burns again and again. LeeLang cried, "Thank God, Mother's home!" I echoed his relief. I knew everything would be all right. Mother would know what to do.

Mother handed the baby to LeeLang. She smeared snake oil (oil she had rendered from snake fat) on my legs and sent a neighbor on his bicycle to the dry-goods shop (they had the only telephone in our area) to call one of Father's friends. The friend was one of those few of our acquaintances who owned a car. Luckily, he was home and came over promptly to drive me and Mother across the river to the hospital.

In the emergency room, nurses removed my sopping wet skirt and placed me on my back on a high padded table. After one quick look that showed me the skin on my thighs and legs had puffed up in huge white blisters, I averted my eyes. I kept them fixed to the white-washed wall while the doctor did things to my legs. Mother told me later that the doctor had snipped with scissors at each blister and peeled away the bloated skin with tweezers, exposing the raw flesh beneath. She shuddered, remembering the sight.

The doctor was a tall northern Indian, with a turban on his head and a curly beard. He said we should not have poured cold water on the burns. This was what had caused the huge blisters. He said we should have used the oil right away or a thick blanket to keep air away from the burns. Medically, he was right, but I am glad CheeLung did pour cold water on me, even if it was the wrong thing to do. There is a comfort, like a friendly voice in the dark, when you are lost in a fog of pain, in action, in someone reacting, knowing what to do, even if it turns out the only thing he knew to do was wrong.

The doctor dressed my burns and wrapped my legs in gauze. He gave Mother some pain pills for me and said I was to come back every day to have my dressings changed. We were driven home by Father's friend, who had most kindly waited for us. I do not recall his name, but I remember his tall lankiness, his young good-natured face showing distress, and his repeated exclamations, "What a terrible thing to happen! It must be so painful. What a terrible thing!"

Father's friend was like Father and his cohorts, a group of fast-talking young men always out for fun, but good-hearted when confronted by another's need. Since I could not walk, he carried me to and from his car's back seat each noon as he chauffeured me and Mother to the hospital for two weeks till my legs healed.

The doctor must have given me a local anesthetic for I did not feel any pain during the skin removal, or on the ride home. In the car Mother rode in the front while I sat with my legs stretched across the entire backseat. I remember thinking the plastic seat smelled strange, but it must have been the ointment from my gauze-wrapped legs. I asked Mother if she had gotten the prize for ChoyChoy at the movie house.

"It was all a sham!" Mother said. I could tell she was angry. I hoped she wasn't angry with me for the trouble I had caused. I hoped the hospital visit had not cost too much. I knew she was always worrying about money. "The manager said they had no prize. He said he didn't know how the rumor got started. But he offered me a free ticket to the show for my having gone to the trouble of coming with the baby. Since I was already there and it was free, I stayed and watched the movie. This is a punishment. This would never have happened if I had not gotten greedy. This is from the gods."

I wasn't sure I followed what she was saying. How could my carelessness with a pot of boiling water be punishment for her? But she was still talking: ". . . thought I would faint when they were ripping the skin off your legs. You were a very brave girl; you didn't make a sound. I would rather suffer five labors and births than go through that hour in the emergency room again."

I felt I had gotten her praise with falsehood. I had not been brave. I had not felt any pain, just numbness during the procedure. But she was telling our driver-friend the whole fiasco of the *Miss ChoyChoy* movie and I was suddenly tired and faint. I slept the rest of the way home.

One of Mother's favorite threats had been "I'm going to skin you" whenever we misbehaved. She never used that threat again. She said, "I never felt what my words meant until I saw what they did."

12

Grandfather Au

Years after Grandfather died, I pieced together the story of his life from things Mother said. He had emigrated from SinWei village in GuangDong Province, China, in search of a better life. He left behind him a wife from an arranged marriage. She farmed the tiny strip of land the family owned and cared for his parents. Arriving in Port Swettenham (now Port Kelang), Malaya, he learned a trade as a ship's carpenter. He fixed leaks on ships plying the spice route between India and China, ships that stopped to load nutmeg, cloves, cinnamon, and pepper in the Celebes and Malaya. Later, he opened a furniture shop in Bunting, a small coastal town about thirty miles from Kelang, our hometown.

Grandfather Au could not persuade his wife to come to him in Malaya. She refused to leave China. He wanted a wife and family. At the end of ten years, he sailed home to China with an ultimatum: "Come with me or I'm taking another wife." His wife agreed to his taking a second wife on condition the new wife accompany him to Malaya and that he continue to send money home to China. She picked a bride for him from her home village; she accepted and drank the traditional cup of tea. That was the last time she saw her husband and his new wife. He faithfully sent money home until she died.

My grandmother, Cheong SiewKeng, was seventeen at the time of her marriage to Grandfather. She bore him three still-born sons and two girls who died in infancy before Mother was born. Mother's birth certificate states that she was born on November 9th, 1928. Mother says she was born at least three months before that. Her Chinese birthdate places her birth in August. Under British rule, births had to be reported within thirty days. It was a long way to the District Officer's town. Grandfather did not want to go to the bother of making the trip until he was sure the baby would live. When she seemed still healthy in December, he reported the birth and picked a random date. This way, he reasoned, the white man was satisfied and he had obeyed the law. It was lucky for Mother that he had done this inconvenient thing. In the 1960s, this piece of paper was the one document which enabled her to obtain citizenship and gain the right for her (and her husband and children) to stay in independent Malaysia, when the government evicted non-natal Malaysians, especially Chinese, in an effort to rid the country of communists.

The three photographs we have of Grandmother Au show a smooth-faced Chinese woman, with hair pulled back tightly in a bun. She looks at us with stern eyes, a grim, unsmiling mouth. The most striking thing about her is her high square forehead. Mother remembers that her mother used to shave that forehead, that she twisted cotton threads round her short hairs to yank them out, to achieve the high-brow, brainy look considered beautiful at the time.

After Mother was born, Grandmother Au lost three more babies before giving birth to a son. My uncle Yuen was a sickly infant and they tried many desperate remedies to hide him from the hungry spirits who were seeking to steal his soul. Once, Mother says, they even hid him all night in the outhouse.

Mother said there were many ways to fool the *thou tzu*, ghosts of women who died in childbirth. One way was to change the child's name to that of an animal like Cat, Dog, Pig, or Cow. Another was to call him by a girl's name like Beautiful Peony, Jade Lotus, or Pearl Lily. Chinese ghosts stole only boy spirits. They had no use for girls.

The third surviving child of my grandparents was a girl. My mother was pregnant with her first child at the time of the birth. Grandmother Au contracted pneumonia after the birth and died shortly thereafter. She was thirty-seven. My baby aunt was a colicky baby and cried constantly. Grandfather, in desperation, gave her to his neighbors, a childless couple. They called her Ah Pao ("Bundle"), because she was such a *hum pao*, bundle of tears.

Grandfather Au came to our house with presents. Always a *kati* of roast pork for Mother, fresh imported fruit for us children. Sometimes it would be grapes the color of jade, cool and sweet. We had to be careful to spit out the seeds—Grandfather said if we swallowed the seeds, a grapevine would sprout in the night from the middle of our foreheads while we slept. Sometimes, he brought big red apples from exotic places like France or America. Or English apple jam, which we would save to eat on fresh bread. Other times, he'd bring oranges. From Jaffa, I knew. They had the word "Jaffa" stamped in purplish-black ink on their skins. Years later, when I visited Israel, I was disappointed to find the old port city of Jaffa had no orange groves, only ancient white stone streets winding up and down its hills. I learned they stamped "Jaffa" on their oranges to show the port of lading.

The only local fruit Grandfather ever brought was the *durian*, the thorny fruit with an incredibly pungent smell. A *durian* is like a leathery green porcupine with sweet golden custard inside. An English writer, Somerset Maugham, once described his experience with the fruit as "eating ambrosia in a public latrine." During *durian* season, we could tell by the smell that Grandfather was coming before he even turned into our lane.

I remember my grandfather as a very tall man. I could be wrong as he died when I was a squirt of eight. To my eyes, he towered over everyone, including my five-foot-three parents. The tight vertical crease between Mother's brows would smooth out when Grandfather visited. He would sit and snooze in the cane easy-chair while I ran my palm over his hair. He kept his hair clipped really short, and it was like feeling newly cut grass.

Grandfather owned a furniture shop in Bunting, near the sea. During school holidays, Brother LeeLang and I would stay with him. He and his son, Uncle Yuen, lived above his furniture shop. Uncle Yuen was only a few years older than Brother LeeLang. We loved playing hide-and-seek with him in the shop. We could hide in pristine cupboards, under shiny wood beds smelling of new sawdust, between chests of drawers and piles of new mattresses in plastic, and over them all hung the pale smooth odor of lacquer. There were glass cabinets for bric-a-brac; there were sets of formica tables and chairs—Grandfather did a lot of business in those. It was the latest technology from the West—stain-proof, scuff-resistant marbleized formica dining sets. Families gleefully moved out their old wood tables for the modern look of pink, or green, formica.

We did not know that formica was low-class, used only for truck-stop diners, kitchen tables, and countertops. Nobody we knew had kitchen counters in those days. We were just moving from the old-fashioned wood stoves to charcoal briquette stoves and all our counters were still fireproof cement or brick.

In the evenings, Grandfather would walk us to the night market for treats like *gado-gado* and *undeh,* sweet rice cakes filled with brown palm sugar. One year, we went several nights to see a performance of the Chinese opera troupe that had come to town. We loved the glitter and glamor of their costumes. We loved the clash of cymbals, the walking in high style to the beat of drums, the romance and the excitement of the plays about emperors and heroic generals. After that vacation, Uncle Yuen and LeeLang said they wanted to be opera stars when they grew up, much to Mother's consternation. "You don't know what a hard life they lead, going from town to town, with no place to call home. You only see the make believe life on the stage! It's not real!"

Grandfather smiled at Mother and told her LeeLang would grow out of his ambition. But he took a stick to Uncle Yuen to beat the nonsense out of him. He never got angry at us, his grandchildren, but he lost his temper easily with his son and often beat him with a stick. Brother and I felt sorry for Uncle Yuen and a little guilty at being glad that Grandfather did not beat us, too.

*My mother
at age 30*

*Mother, age 10,
in her family
photograph, 1938*

Grandmother Au
with baby Uncle Yuen

Grandfather's Favoritism

My uncle Yuen suspected his father
of favoritism, even from the grave.
Bull-headed men, they never gave,
wanted only to dominate. Uncle forbade
Mother to visit their father's grave
with food and other offerings needed
by the Chinese dead, in case she got
a larger share of ancestral luck.

My mother obeyed his injunction for four
years, till she dreamt her father in rags,
housed in a mud hut with holes for window
and door, his needs forgotten by his son.
That week she made a bonfire in our yard,
by its flames, dispatched a paper mansion,
furniture, a million Bank of Hell dollars.

Later, she dreamt him happy in his new house.
My uncle visits once a year. He blames
her still for parental love he couldn't win.

—from *Men & Other Strange Myths*

13

Grandmother Tries to Give My Sisters Away

My mother was pregnant with her first child when she received word that her mother had contracted pneumonia. When she asked her mother-in-law for permission to go to Port Swettenham (eight miles away) to see her mother, Grandmother Tham said, "No, there's too much work here. It's just woman's sickness after birthing a baby." Grandmother Au had given birth to her third surviving child a few months earlier. When Grandfather Au sent word of the death, Grandmother Tham would not allow Mother to attend the funeral. She said attending a funeral might have adverse effects on the Tham grandson my mother was carrying. She was taking no chances with her grandson.

I shudder to think how my mother would have suffered at Grandmother Tham's hands if I had been her first child. Luckily, her firstborn was a boy, my brother LeeLang (Priority Ability), so Grandmother was pleased. I know she scolded for a day and a night after I was born. "A girl, a good-for-nothing girl." My father was pleased. He named me ChoyKam (Jadegreen Harp) after an old girl-friend, a fact Mother angrily discovered years later.

Mother's next child was a girl, my sister ChoyMui (Jadegreen Plumblossom). Grandmother grumbled about how she had known from the matchmaker's photograph that Mother was too thin to bear sons. My sister ChoyMui died at age three. Luckily, my brother

CheeLung (Fortunate Ability) came along next. This pacified Grandmother for a while.

Before the next two babies were born, Grandmother spoke long and earnestly to Father every night as we ate our rice at the kitchen table. She talked about the advantages of giving up the new baby, if it was a girl, for adoption. "On your salary, you have to be realistic. We are too poor to feed so many mouths, especially useless girls' mouths. Cousin Wong is an old maid; she is looking for a girl to adopt. She is rich; she works in a bank. The baby will have a good home, meat for dinner. It's not giving her away for real—she'll still be a relative."

I wondered how Grandmother could be such an unnatural woman. I knew she herself had once been pregnant and carried a child to term. Unfortunately, the baby, a girl, had been stillborn. She had not conceived again. My father had been adopted after she gave up hope of bearing her own son. I once asked Mother how was it possible that Grandmother hated girls. After all, she too was a woman and a girl once. Mother said, "Your grandmother never learned to think for herself. She just repeats things she's heard rich relatives say. She thinks they must be right if they're rich. A lot of people in the world are like that."

I watched Father's face as he shoveled rice into his mouth, his eyes giving no clue to how he felt about Grandmother's proposal. I could not bear it if he agreed with Grandmother, I thought. It would mean he did not love me, a girl-child; it would mean that only the chance of birth order had kept me in the family. I did not look at Mother because I knew how she felt. She was angry and frightened, desperate to keep the baby she was carrying in her womb. She stayed silent while Grandmother dripped her poison in Father's ear. If she argued with Grandmother at the dinner table, Father would get up and leave. He hated dissension and loud arguments. She would talk to Father, try to persuade him to keep the baby, in the privacy of their bedroom when he came home late at night. Because Grandmother was the matriarch, Mother could not tell her to shut up. All power over our lives resided in Father's hands. Mother could only influence his decisions. It helped her greatly that ChoyNgor (Jadegreen Lady-in-the-Moon) was a beautiful baby from birth and resembled the sister who had died, with large eyes and a high nose. Father took a fancy to her and was easily persuaded to dismiss his mother's machinations to give the baby to the wealthy childless cousin.

When she became pregnant again, Mother knew she would have trouble keeping the next baby if it was a girl. She had heard about tubal ligation, and how educated women were having their tubes tied after two or three children. She persuaded Father to sign the doctor's form that gave his permission for her to have her tubes tied immediately after her next delivery. With that done, she could argue that this was her last baby and should not be given away. Father was in the throes of a new romance and only came to the hospital once to see the baby. Worn out with winning the struggle to keep her child, Mother did not bother with thinking up a fancy name for her. She named her ChoyChoy (Jadegreen Jadegreen) to round things off.

May Means Beautiful in Chinese

We name daughters
Yee May, Soo May, Yin May, May May,
May Wan, May Choo, May Li, as if
Beauty is the main imperative
for a woman, as if the naming
will make it fact. We load a diversity
of hopes on sons: Ying for courage,
Ming for brilliance, Fook for fortune,
Tai for greatness, and for honor
and endurance, Chong Yan.

Only when bad luck demons pester
a son with sickness and accidents do
we hide his maleness, call him Cat
or Dog. Ah Mow and Ah Gow are common
life-saving names. If this ploy fails,
there's one sure way to turn away a demon:
disguise your son's value behind a girl's
name, call him Beautiful.

—from *Bad Names for Women*

*Mother and Grandmother Tham
on a good day*

14
Jadegreen Plumblossom

One of my earliest memories is playing with my little sister ChoyMui (Jadegreen Plumblossom). Father would hold a board at an angle to make a slope and she and I would race little lead cars down it. When ChoyMui died at the age of three, Grandmother took me and Elder Brother LeeLang over to Grand-Aunt One's house. When we came home, she was gone. All her clothes and bedding too, were gone. Her name was never mentioned in our house. It was as if she had never existed. But I knew she had lived from my memories of playing with her, from the emptied look in Mother's eyes the rare times she allowed herself to rest from housework and tending to Grandmother's demands. Then, she would sit in the cane chair and stare out the door at the red-dirt lane.

I was only six years old then, but I remembered the hole she left, the hole that swallowed all the questions I wanted to ask. I remembered her round face, big eyes, her almost bald head with its soft downy fuzz of hair. I thought of her often, the little sister who vanished so suddenly from our house, our lives, like a leaf fallen and trodden under by careless feet. I think I resented the family acting as if ChoyMui had never been. Mortality, dying, and leaving no trace of having existed became a constant frame for the events of my life. When I began writing poems, part of the fierce joy I found in the act came from the feeling that I was defying death's eraser; I was leaving signs that I had lived, hoping someone coming along later would find my work, like signposts in a foggy night, helpful and comforting if lost.

It is the custom for Chinese families to *han shan*, walk the mountains, in the fourth lunar month to visit the graves of ancestors. They bring food and wine, Bank of Hell money, and grass cutters to clean and tend the graves and satisfy the financial and culinary needs of the dead.

For us as children, ChingMing (Clear Bright) festival was always a cheerful occasion; a time to visit grandparents and to picnic on the hills where Chinese cemeteries are usually located. We'd climb the hills trying to remember from last year's visit the way to a grandparent's grave, showing off by leading the way. I remember LeeLang and I leaping and racing each other up steep slopes, exulting in our agility and the challenge of the rough terrain, just glad to be alive and not yet lying under grassy mounds with gravestones. We visited my mother's parents' graves. Father's mother was living and his father was buried in faraway Hong Kong. Mother said, "The gods know if his grave is still there. I hear there's a big highway where half the cemetery used to be."

At each grave we visited, Mother would sweep the stone altar clear of leaves, debris, and dirt, and spread out the food offerings. She'd light incense sticks and red candles and burn Bank of Hell money and silver and gold ingots made of paper, and pour cups of tea and wine into the earth for the grandparent in that grave as well as the guardian gods of the hill. We children were assigned the task of clipping the grass grown high over the grave mound. Then we would fan out gold and silver joss papers, set them on the grave mound, and weigh them down with stones to keep them from blowing away. It was always windy on cemetery hill. Then we were free to run about the hilltop and pretend we were birds flying from grave to grave.

Since Father was not related by blood to Mother's parents, he did not have to pray at their graves. He would walk about, looking at gravestones. Sometimes, he'd call out to Mother that he had found a name he recognized or had known. Or he'd take his Chinese newspaper and wander off to find a place to sit and read.

Invariably, Mother would look up and notice him. "Aiiyaaah! He's sitting on someone's tombstone! He's offending the spirit!" After the praying was done, Father would come back and eat with us. Often, he'd come back before the praying was done and say,

"Hurry up! Spirits don't take that long to eat. I'm hungry."

Before we packed up and left, Mother would clamber over to the tombstone Father had used as a seat and offer joss sticks and prayers for forgiveness for her husband's thoughtlessness and lack of respect. "You don't want to offend a spirit," Mother explained to us children. "Besides which, it isn't respectful. Would you plop your backside on a living person's face? Just because they're dead is no reason to treat them differently."

Years later, as we trudged with our supplies from Grandmother Au's grave toward Grandfather Au's on the next hill, I asked Mother where my little sister was buried. She pointed to a distant area on the lower slopes. It was a wire-fenced field of tall grass and weeds.

"Can I go and see her grave?" I asked.

Mother shook her head. She said, "They don't have markers in the children's field."

"Don't you remember from her funeral?" I persisted.

"The undertaker took her away. We don't have funerals for children," Mother said, her tone warning me to leave her alone.

Later, I learned that the souls of deceased male children were given a place in the ancestral tablet on the family altar and received part of descendants' offerings. And that the souls of deceased unmarried daughters were left out in the cold, due to the Chinese practice of patrilineal descent. Only when a girl is married does she acquire a rightful place in her husband's ancestral tablet, especially if she produces male offspring. It angered me that my sister was not included in our family tablet because she had been born a girl. And died before marriage.

It was only in recent years that Mother could talk about our dead sister. It turned out that Brother LeeLang, too, had asked about her. The younger children born after her had been barely aware of her existence; they only knew there had been a sister preceding them because the next girl child could not be addressed as Second Sister.

As adults, LeeLang and I compared memories and the few answers we each had managed to extract. We found we had very different versions of our sister's death.

LeeLang had been told by Mother that ChoyMui died from stepping on a rusty nail and the subsequent infection and fever. Mother blamed Father for saying he was too busy when she asked him to take their feverish child to the doctor. "Must have been tetanus," LeeLang said.

Mother had told me that ChoyMui had been a timid child and that her spirit had been frightened at the funeral of Great Grand-Aunt Three, loosening its hold on the flesh, and that she had died a week later. When LeeLang and I together asked her which version was correct, she gave us a third story.

ChoyMui had had an epileptic fit and fainted. She and grandmother had applied smelling salts in a wad of cotton to her nose. "We were stupid and ignorant fools," Mother said, "we did not know to remove the pad from her nose. I'm sure the poor baby died from lack of air to breathe."

LeeLang and I looked at each other. Mother had amazed us beyond words, again.

Later, LeeLang said, "Mother doesn't know the cause of death. She's just guessing." I agreed with him. I think that my mother kept seeking an answer for the loss of her daughter, that she believed different things at different times, blaming Father, Great Grand-Aunt Three's ghost, and herself in turn as she grieved for her child. It might have been better if she had been allowed to talk about her grief, but our culture did not allow it.

Her guilt now centers on the name she gave our sister. When Father died, she had to place an obituary in the Chinese papers. When she listed (as required) the deceased's children, dead and alive, the newspaper's obituary editor had exclaimed, "No wonder she's dead. With a name like that, 'Friable and Rotting,' of course she wouldn't live long!" Mother told us this later. "I never thought of it but it's true! The homophones for Choy and Mui are 'crunchy' and 'decaying.' I only thought that Jadegreen Plumblossom was such a pretty name, I thought it suited her, she was such a beautiful baby! If only I had named her a more auspicious name, she might still be alive!"

Walking in the mountains:
Visiting Grandmother Tham at her grave in the spring.
Mother in a hurry with incense sticks

15

The Nuns

My earliest ambition was to become a nun. All the people I admired were Irish nuns in the Convent School I attended. Covered from head to ankle in white, the color of goodness, their coifs, wimples, and habits always pristine and pure, nuns walked in their men's leather shoes and sensible cotton socks swiftly and lightly through my dreams of a future I desired. Sister Louis, Sister Jerome, Sister Clara, Reverend Mother Aidan, Sister Michael—their names were a litany that meant peace, pools of shade in the too-hot Malaysian sun. They were never ruffled by screaming kids, fighting parents, malicious grandmothers. After the day's teaching, they vanished into the residential wing of the Convent of the Holy Infant Jesus, next to the chapel where we students were allowed to go and pray. I would see them at their windows, heads bent over a book. They had books to read. They had time to read. Their lives seemed like heaven to me.

I penetrated that holy of holies, their sleeping quarters, once, when I was sent with an urgent message for Reverend Mother Rita, the headmistress who replaced Reverend Mother Aidan after she returned to Ireland. Each bedroom was as I had imagined, a small narrow room with a window to the sky, a narrow bed with pure white sheets, a small bedside table with a clock, a crucifix, and a missal prayerbook, and a wooden *almari* (wardrobe). I knew white habits hung serenely in it. And everywhere, like morning light, lay total silence, the utmost peace. Staring at the pocket of privacy, I yearned to possess it. I, who shared a room with brothers and sisters, who had never had a room of my own, coveted it and knew I sinned.

Sister Clara was the cook and the only nun who ever got her whites a little soiled. But she was always cheerful and kind and gave us a banana to eat if we brought a message to her kitchen. I was always happy to be sent to the kitchen for fruit or flowers for still-life art classes.

Sister Louis taught me needlework in grades four and five. I was terrible at the subject. I seemed to spend half my time in her class undoing the stitches I had just wrought with many prickings of my fingers and an intense desire to please. Sister Louis talked about the need to learn her skills. "Someday, you will all be wives and mothers. A good wife, a good mother must know how to sew and cook. She must be Modest!" Modesty was a favorite topic of Sister Louis's lectures. She was aghast at the modern *cheongsam*, the Chinese national costume with side-slits. The slits had risen to heights most alarming to Sister Louis. She warned us constantly not to wear *cheongsams* with "indecent" slits, which she demonstrated by drawing her finger from the approximate location of her knee up to her hip, decorously covered by layers of her ankle-length habit. Sister Louis rolled her eyes and pantomimed her shock and fainting should she ever see us in one of the "indecent" things. She made us laugh and we promised her we would not shock her, ever.

Sister Louis knew we were "good girls." To make sure we stayed so, she told us often the many rules of behavior for good girls.

Good girls always sit with their knees together. They never sit with their knees apart.

Good girls never cross their legs. (Especially not wearing slitted *cheongsams*.)

Good girls never shake their legs or wriggle in their chairs from impatience. Drawing attention to their bodies is something good girls never do.

Good girls never look down at the bathwater when stepping into the bath (in case you caught a glimpse of naked nether parts). Sister Louis need not have worried about this—everyone in our class lived in a house without a Western-style bathtub. We dipped water from a storage jar and poured it over ourselves.

Sister Louis had a vivacity, a lively way of speaking. We never tired of listening to the Irish lilt of her voice. She talked constantly with her hands as well as with her tongue. She acted out everything she said, with exaggerated mimes that delighted us. She was brimming over with life and energy and enthusiasm. By contrast, all the wives and mothers I knew were tired, worn-out, often bad-tempered, generally unhappy women. I knew I did not want to be a wife and mother when I grew up. I wanted to be full of vitality and rich with knowledge, to be full of delight in what I did, like Sister Louis. *Ergo*, I wanted to be a nun.

Since I wasn't going to be a wife and mother, it didn't matter if I couldn't sew. I gave in to impatience and took scissors to the embroidered rose-petal I had been told to undo. Snip, snip, snip. There, all the crimson threads came away easily. So did a snippet of cloth. I had cut a hole in the pillowcase! Luckily for me, Mother was a good wife and mother. She patched the hole and embroidered a bigger rose petal over it so cleverly that Sister Louis never knew there was a hole there.

Reverend Mother Aidan was the headmistress of the school in my early years. She was a tiny woman with a soft burry voice. But when she spoke, everyone listened. All the teachers and Sisters respected her and deferred to her. "Yes, Reverend Mother," "Certainly, Reverend Mother," "I'll see to it right away, Reverend Mother." She was a woman who held power, a rare thing in my world.

Sister Michael taught English in the upper grades. She looked like the plaster angels atop the columns in the church. She had bright blue eyes and a pink and white complexion, and our rare glimpses of her hair that strayed from under her coif glinted gold among the gray. The girls whispered that Sister Michael's fiancé had been a pilot shot down and killed in the war and she had become a nun after losing him. We sighed at the thought of the romantic rumor but no one was crass enough to mention it to her. Sister Michael was also Irish and full of energy. She directed plays and helped us build and paint stage sets for them. She had a fondness for Shakespeare and made us learn *Julius Caesar* by heart. To this day, I can recite chunks of that play.

Let me have men about me that are fat.
Yon Cassius has a lean and hungry look.
He thinks too much. Such men are dangerous.

To us, students in a girls' school, taught only by women, all men were strange and dangerous. It seems a contradiction, now, that we were being groomed for marriage and motherhood by nuns, women who had forsworn both. Yet the method seemed to work well enough. Most of us who passed through Sister Louis's hands did become wives and mothers. I joined the majority, though I fell from grace many times and even wore the high-slitted *cheongsam* and miniskirts in college. But Sister Louis had long departed the shores of Malaysia and was not there to roll her eyes and fall down in shock at such immodesty.

16

Of Monks & Feet

Poetic truth is a slippery slope kind of balancing act. The writer takes facts and events and uses selected elements from them. Sometimes, the poem is a response to an actual event, an acting out of "I wish I had said this, or done that." This was the case with my first Mrs. Wei poem: "Mrs. Wei on the Bus."

Mrs. Wei on the Bus

found a seat thankfully set down her bags.
Hot bodies jostled her: schoolgirls in blue,
women shoppers, salesmen, a Buddhist

monk carrying his alms pouch. A schoolgirl
near him struggled toward the exit.
She stumbled over Mrs. Wei's bags.

Mrs. Wei helped her up. "Why are you
leaving? You just got on. Are you
feeling sick?"

Eyes wide, the girl shook her head.
"No—the Monk—he touched me.
I'll catch the next bus."

Mrs. Wei rose in wrath, hissed to the girl
to watch her bags and began to bellow.
"Lecher! Animal! Reptile in saffron robe!

Secret Eater of Forbidden Meat!
Molesting young girls on buses!
I'll report you to your Abbot,

you vomit on Buddha's face!"
Eyes turned. Heads turned. In silence,
he took the path that opened to the exit.

"Always carry a safety pin," Mrs. Wei said
to the schoolgirl, "When scum like that
surfaces, stab it in the ass.

That jackal is going to be
a lizard in his next life.
May Lord Buddha have mercy on his soul."

—from *Paper Boats*

A friend and I had a similar encounter with a lascivious
Buddhist monk when we were fifteen. Since we lacked the boldness
and experience of "Mrs. Wei," we beat a hasty retreat from his wandering hands to the front of the bus. We wished we had had a better
way to deal with the situation. Our retreat left us humiliated and
dissatisfied. When I told my mother about the incident, she reacted
in the spirit of Mrs. Wei. "Use words, loud words, to draw everyone's attention on him and shame him. He is a disgrace to his god!
In future, carry a nail file and jab it into that fatherless turtle's egg.
That'll teach him to keep his hands to himself."

It was twenty years later, after I married and came to America
where I encountered the concepts of the "Jewish Mother" and the
"Italian Mother," that I felt a need to write about the quintessential
"Chinese Mother," and the poem came to me, almost fully formed. I

went on to write many more Mrs. Wei poems, but the subsequent poems are in the first person: Mrs. Wei speaks for herself.

The popularity of Mrs. Wei is something of a puzzle to me. The Mrs. Wei poems are not lyrical, nor poetic per se. I think it is the motherly voice of experience, the down-to-earth, yet superstitious, sometimes shrill, always pragmatic, outspoken and definitely not politically correct persona that appeals to everyone. I have been asked many times, "Whom did you base Mrs. Wei on?" I always answer truthfully that she is a blend of much of my own mother and other Chinese mothers I have known.

Calling a spade a spade is common to most Chinese mothers. The first time I revisited Malaysia after living in America, an aunt exclaimed upon seeing me, "People go to America and come back pale and fair. You go to America and come back sunburned like a *lye-shui mui,* a drag-earth-water coolie-girl!" (The lowest form of work for women is on construction sites, carrying bricks and buckets of freshly mixed cement. Toiling long days in the hot sun, these laborers acquire tans that would be the envy of any Westerner, tans despised by Malaysians who covet the beautiful indoor pallor of white-collar workers.)

I fully agree with the poet who said that "Poetry does not have to be truth. It must only feel like the truth." A faithful rendering of what actually happened seldom makes a good poem. For me, poetry is the shaping of selected elements of reality with the imagined, to reach an articulation of a truth of human existence.

The one poem where I had to sacrifice truth to achieve poetic truth is my "Golden Lilies," an early poem about the ancient Chinese practice of foot-binding. This atrocious custom inflicted on female children spread as a mark of gentility and upper-class status, and was prevalent from the time of the early Sung emperors till the 1900s. Girls whose feet were not bound could not hope to achieve a good marriage and were subjected to the scorn and taunts of the community. Only peasants (who needed their daughters able-bodied to help with farming), hill tribes, and other "uncivilized" groups avoided binding their daughters' feet. The mutilated feet, kept in bindings of silk and embroidered velvet shoes, were called "golden lotus" or "golden lilies" (*chin-lien*) and were extolled and praised in poems and essays by male enthusiasts. Su Tung-p'o (1036–1101) said some romantic things about bound feet.

Anointed with fragrance, she takes lotus steps;
Though often sad, she steps with swift lightness.
She dances like the wind, leaving no physical trace.
Another stealthily but happily tries on the palace style,
But feels such distress when she tries to walk!
Look at them in the palms of your hands,
      so wondrously small that
they defy description.

So I wrote my own modern-day, woman's-perspective poem on the subject.

Golden Lilies

Grandmother could swear the air purple
and black. My parents became
meeker than white mice when she
stamped her foot in anger.
She had tiny feet and wore size four
in children's shoes.

She hated hospitals. Their smells
snarled and trapped her again
in the childhood terror when
the footbinder smashed a mallet
on her toes, crushed her feet,
squeezed them into taut red silk strips
that were tightened each week.
The smell of decay
meshed with the pain forever
and hospital smells triggered
agony in her mind's unbound flesh.

                                      —from *Paper Boats*

Today, I would re-title this poem "Cousin Yong on Golden Lilies." The part that bothers me about this poem is that the grandmother in the poem is not my grandmother. She was my grand-aunt. But the poem would not work with "My grand-aunt's feet . . ." The poem required an immediacy of tone that rejected "grand-aunt." So I used "grandmother," and lied for the sake of "poetic truth." My fierce little grandmother never permitted her feet to be bound. She was the youngest of three daughters. Her mother had died before she reached the age of foot-binding. Though her sisters had bound feet, grandmother rejected the foot-binder so violently that her father and aunts did not have the will to enforce the tradition on her. Luckily, she had naturally small feet, and the matchmaker was able to find her a good match, despite her two handicaps of unbound feet and of being born in the year of the tiger. Families with boys born in the years of the rabbit, sheep, mouse, ox, or pig slammed their doors quickly on a matchmaker calling out the virtues of a tiger.

17

The Corner Coffee Shop

Though we were poor, my mother managed to contrive treats for us children. Once a month or sometimes twice, she produced thirty cents and sent me on my bicycle down to the coffee shop at the junction of Meru Road and Kapar Road. We knew that their bread finished baking at three o'clock and we could get a hot crusty loaf then, with a paper of *kaya*, a sweet syrupy jam made of eggs and coconut milk. That was just enough for a thick slice for everyone in the family. On even rarer occasions, she had another twenty-five cents for a stick of butter (Fernleaf brand all the way from New Zealand) that we spread on the bread and gobbled up with great relish. Oh, the golden and rare taste of butter! No butter and bread has ever tasted as wonderful as those seldom and special feasts of childhood.

The only thing I disliked about going to the corner coffee shop was my fear of running into Ah Peng, the "crazy woman." I never knew if she would ignore me (which I fervently hoped for) or if she would start shouting at me, accusing me of wanting to steal her baby. Ah Peng was a middle-aged woman with wild tangled hair and huge staring eyes. She wore loose black pants and baggy white blouses that were always coffee-stained. Her bare feet in rubber slippers were grimy and she had dirt in her nails. Her "baby" was a much-scuffed rubber doll with hardly any face left and just a few strands of black hair. Ah Peng would clutch it and croon to it or, forgetting it, drop it in the dirt. There it would lie until she would miss it and have hysterics, crying that someone had kidnapped her "baby." Then her parents (who owned the coffee shop) and all the waiters would hunt all over the shop and environs for it.

"Poor Ah Peng was not always a crazy woman," Mother said. She remembered when Ah Peng was a sweet simpleminded child, liking everyone and eager to please. Mother remembered her sitting at a table in the coffee shop, happily playing with her coloring books and pencils for hours. When her body ripened, though her mind never did, an unknown man took advantage of her and got her pregnant. Despite long and persistent questioning by her parents, she could not tell them who was responsible for her condition. She simply did not remember events beyond their occurrence. Even then, she did not become wary of people. She still trusted everyone and would do whatever anybody suggested to her.

Everyone knew some scoundrel had taken advantage of poor Ah Peng. Mr. and Mrs. Chan could not hide their daughter's condition. The simple girl clapped her hands and laughed when she finally understood Mrs. Chan's explanation. She told all the customers in the coffee shop that she was going to have her own baby. Ah Peng liked babies. Sometimes, kind Mrs. Liu next door would let her push her baby in its carriage. And Mrs. Mah across the street had a baby, though she did not like Ah Peng touching her baby.

Ah Peng had an easy delivery. The Chans declared they would raise their grandson as their own and hoped they would live long enough to complete their task. Meanwhile, they hovered over him, searching for comfort, little signs to show normal intelligence. Ah Peng gave him her favorite coloring pencils. She cried when her mother took them away from the infant.

Mother remembered how everyone said the gods were kind when the month-old baby died in his sleep. Ah Peng screamed for hours after the undertaker took the little bundled-up body away. For the first time in her life, she did not greet people with a beaming smile. And she did not forget. She grew sullen and suspicious. Mrs. Chan could not divert her with the usual cakes and lollipops. Then Ah Peng began to steal babies.

The first time, it was Mrs. Liu's baby. The Liu family agreed not to call the police after the Chans found Ah Peng cowering with the sleeping baby in her room right away and returned the baby safely. A week later, Ah Peng stole the Mah baby. Mr. Mah was less forgiving than the Liu's. He called the police and Ah Peng was sent to faraway Tanjong Rambutan, the asylum for the insane. Two years later, Ah Peng was pronounced cured and came home with a substitute "baby," a rubber doll she cradled in her arms and rocked constantly. She no longer stole babies. But she would break out every now and then and accuse strangers of trying to steal her "baby."

I was afraid of Ah Peng. I was afraid of the holes that were her eyes; they swallowed up the rules of the ordinary world I lived in. When I spoke to her, my words broke on the blankness of her stare and fell, emptied of meaning. They were all the tools I knew and believed in. The hint in Ah Peng's eyes of a vast hungering need, an existence seeking, lacking meaning, was something I could not bear to acknowledge.

18

The Hole in the Wall

I was nine and it was my first visit to Kuala Lumpur, our capital. I was scared. I held tight to Grandmother's hand as she led me and Brother LeeLang across streets with cars roaring down on us from both directions, belching smoke and brakes squealing. Since we got off the bus from Kelang, I had been worried by the noise and the sense of urgency that seemed to come from the hot pavement and the click-clacking, thrump-thumping feet of people pressing against us. I was glad when we were safely in the dim stairwell leading up to our cousins' apartment.

Our cousins lived above their hardware shop on Ampang Road, one of the quiet sections of Kuala Lumpur, they said. From the relative peace of their upstairs window I looked down on the bus station and streets below. It made me think of ants rushing to and from a handful of crumbs back to the hill. I do not remember much of the town besides this impression of urgent hurry and noise, and quiet days indoors. My newly met cousins were WahChai (a nine-year-old boy), KeatWah, and YatWah (seven- and five-year-old girls). Their father, Cousin-Uncle YeeFong, and their mother, Cousin-Auntie, whose name I never knew, took us for walks on their street in the evenings.

The shops on Ampang Road were like the shops on our main street except there were more of them and they were more crowded. One shop stood out as very strange. It was very quiet; its interior,

seen through a small doorway, was dim and seemed to have almost
no customers. It was the *chattiahs'* shop, my cousins said. Inside
were two rows of *chattiahs*, Indian moneylenders. My mother sometimes said that if things got really bad, we would be forced to go to
the *chattiahs*. She said this in a tone that meant a fate most dire and
to be avoided. Curious to finally see the dreaded *chattiahs*, I looked
in and saw dark southern Indian men wearing white Western shirts
over *dhotis*, white cotton wraparound cloths. They sat, facing each
other, in lotus position like carved buddhas in the temple. Each had,
before him, a low heavy wooden table with a thick ledger on it and a
pen. I was disappointed not to see boxes of money. I never saw any
activity in the shop. Cousin-Uncle YeeFong said they were like
banks and made money from lending money at reasonable rates to
fellow Indians and unreasonable rates to non-Indians. I thought they
seemed dull for bogeymen.

The best part of our visit was the excursion to Bukit Bintang
(Star Hill) Amusement Park. It was Saturday night, the last night of
our visit. The park was crowded with people jostling for a turn on
the two roller coasters and the dodge 'em cars. There were also
skeeball galleries, games stalls, and food stalls. I was entranced by
the prizes on display, tiers of plastic dolls with lifelike faces and gor-
geous frilly dresses, and stuffed animals in fantasy colors—blue
dogs, pink bears, orange cats, green monkeys. The air was rich with
smells of soy sauce noodles, roasting pork, coconut cakes. Our
Saturday-night bazaar was a dull affair compared to this.

Cousin-Uncle YeeFong bought us sticks of *satay*, marinated
beef slivers on bamboo skewers grilled over red-hot coals. I liked
Cousin-Uncle YeeFong. He was a big, quiet man who looked as if he
had just gotten out of bed and was longing to go back. His eyes were
always half closed. He bought us bouffant balls of pink cotton candy
as we strolled through the park, we children running ahead, our
grandmother and his mother (who had bound feet and used a cane)
pacing slowly behind.

As we passed a huge wooden building adjoining the park,
Cousin WahChai beckoned us to join him at a tiny hole he had found
in the wall. We could hear music and bursts of applause. We took
turns by age. When it was my turn to put my eye to the hole, I saw a
big hall filled with tables at which men sat, smoking and drinking.
They all had their heads turned toward a nearby stage. A woman
was dancing. She wore bright-colored scarves. She kept losing

scarves as she danced. I could see one of her breasts. It was exposed except for the nipple which was covered by a tinfoil star. A little man jumped onto the stage from a table near the band. He began picking up the dropped scarves. The woman danced over to him with a radiant smile. Then, with a hard thrust of her hip, in time to a drumroll, she bumped him off the stage. He fell with a comically dismayed look on his face and got a huge laugh and cheers from the audience. By this time, the dancer had lost all her scarves save for a little one across her bottom. I had never seen so much nude flesh before.

The next thing I knew, my eye was no longer at the peephole. Cousin-Uncle YeeFong had picked me up and deposited me a foot away from the wall. He smiled at me and said, "My turn." He bent his ponderous frame and glued his eye to the hole. He stayed bent for a long time. Brother and Cousin WahChai were giggling muffled boy jokes to each other as they searched further along the wall for another peephole. I stood with my girl cousins waiting for their turn to look. I wondered what the dancer would do now that she had no more scarves to lose. The music was still playing. Was she dancing naked? Wasn't she ashamed to have no clothes on in public?

Cousin-Uncle YeeFong was still bent over with his eye to the hole in the wall. He would not budge despite his two daughters tugging at him and insisting it was their turn, they hadn't had a look yet. A few passers-by stopped in curiosity. They too wanted a look. Cousin-Uncle ignored them. I think he would have stayed there all night if his mother, Grand-Aunt Yau, had not come up. She seemed to know what was going on. All at once, Cousin-Uncle had straightened up with a yelp and a hand to his buttocks. His old mother had jabbed his rear with her walking stick. "You turtle's egg, showing such a bad example to the children! Come along now, all of you." I realized I had done a "bad" thing. I knew it from the look on Cousin-Uncle's reddened face as we followed Grand-Aunt's indignantly stiff back all the way home.

A few weeks later, I overheard my father and Cousin-Uncle YeeFong talking about the hole-in-the-wall escapade and began to understand it was not the looking at a naked woman that had made him ashamed; it was being caught by his mother.

Father: You mean you actually saw Rose Chan, the stripper? She is red-hot; her show's been sold out for months! What was she like?

YeeFong (cupping his hands six inches before his chest): Her breasts were this big! And her buttocks were like twin moons, white as silken tofu. Looking at her made my mouth water . . .

Father: Talking about her is making you drool now!

YeeFong: If you had seen her, you'd drool too. I went back the next night but they had boarded up the hole. Too many people found it after us, I guess.

At this point, they noticed me behind the door and took their conversation with them for a long walk. I stared after their backs, wondering why the sight of an overweight naked woman should make Cousin-Uncle YeeFong's eyes open and shine.

Mrs. Wei and Modern Marriage

Nowadays people are more romantic;
they kiss and cuddle even after
marriage. It looks very nice.

The men of my generation
kiss only low women. Couples
are water buffalo in a plow.

Now plows are easily dropped,
the buffalo run wild after kissing
while we stay in our fields.

Mr. Wei and I have never kissed.
Luckily, he is more interested
in high cuisine than low women.

—from *Paper Boats*

19

The Bad Widow

Mother told us to beware of dogs, especially strays. The danger of rabies was a very real thing in Malaysia, where stray dogs roamed the town, garnishing a living from leftovers discarded by street hawkers and food stalls. She became paranoid about chasing dogs away from the house with a broom after the ice-cream seller, Mr. Ho, died.

Mr. Ho lived in the house next to the little temple at the end of our lane. He had seven children. His wife took in laundry and their yard was always filled with clotheslines and clothes drying in the hot sun. Any time I walked past their house, I could see Mrs. Ho bent over a table, ironing. There would be a charcoal brazier burning, with glowing coals for refilling her heavy black iron and piles of neatly folded clothes. Her older children delivered the bundles of clothes each evening to the twelve families from whom they picked up the next day's wash.

Mrs. Ho told Mother she stretched her budget by feeding her children lunches of rice with a spoon of cheap Planta margarine and soy sauce. Inspired by this, Mother bought a big can of Planta margarine. We hated the taste of it on our rice. Mother couldn't insist on it. She hated it on rice too. And bread cost too much. Mother made herself eat rice with margarine until she finished the can. She never bought Planta margarine again.

One rainy afternoon, Mr. Ho came home with a puppy he had

found by the roadside. The puppy was greeted with joy by his children. Mrs. Ho was not happy. She complained about the cost of feeding a hungry, growing monster of a dog. "Easy for Ho to say, 'Feed the dog our leftovers.' We never have leftovers."

Two weeks later, we heard Mr. Ho was in the hospital. The puppy had bitten him and he was dying of rabies, in spite of eighteen painful injections in his stomach. Mrs. Ho said he was foaming at the mouth and didn't recognize her or the children. The dog was taken away by police and shot. Mr. Ho died. Mrs. Ho came to borrow money. The coffin, the burial plot, the paper gold and silver ingots, the Bank of Hell money, candles and joss sticks, and the Taoist priest to chant Mr. Ho's way across the Yellow Springs to the Underworld had wiped out her savings. Luckily, the Funeral Supply Store had let her have the mourning clothes and sackcloth hoods for the funeral on credit. Father went fund-raising for her. He got her story "Mad dog bites man: widow left destitute with seven children" in the national papers. Contributions began pouring in. Mrs. Ho began to sleep at night; she stopped looking old. She took in extra washing, adding two more families. She moved into the children's room and rented out her bedroom. She stopped coming to tell Mother her troubles.

A year later, the rumors began. Ah Por, the old woman from the temple, told everyone Mrs. Ho's recent behavior was unbecoming to a chaste widow. She and her lodger, a young man, were laughing too loudly and too often together. She was buying chicken to make dinner for him; she was buying eggs for his breakfast. She was teaching him to make ice cream so he could quit his job as a waiter and set up in Ho's old business.

All the neighbors listened and talked about it. "Ho must be tossing and turning in his grave. A widow must be chaste and cold. She must mind the good name of her dead husband." Grandmother was especially loud in her disapproval. "I was widowed at thirty. I never looked at a man since that day. I have been a good widow. I can look the Tham ancestors in the face when I cross the Yellow Springs."

I did not know Mrs. Ho well. I only knew she was a quiet, hard-working woman, with an odd liking for margarine and rice, that her children were quiet and serious and polite and went to Chinese schools. I thought Chinese custom was hard, requiring a woman to stop being alive if she had the misfortune to lose her husband young. I hoped she and the lodger would get married and become respectable so the lane would stop being outraged and titillated by Ah Por's reports. It was not to be.

Two years later, the lodger disappeared with Mrs. Ho's money. She grew quieter, and harsher with her children. "Serves her right," said Ah Por from the temple. "The poor thing! Men cannot be trusted. I could have told her that if she had bothered to ask for my advice."

Long after I left our lane, I remembered the abandoned widow, could still visualize the small, thin woman who had gambled for love and lost. I remembered her pinched face, pinched lips, the aura of sorrow, as she stood over her ironing, sprinkling water on a white shirt, testing her iron on a waxy banana leaf before pressing out the creases in the pristine white cotton. I heard that her children left home, left her as soon as they could earn their keep. I knew they had adored their father, loved the ungrateful puppy he gave them. I can only guess that they abandoned their mother because she had abandoned them in her heart long ago, for a stray man she had loved more than she loved them, for a stray that had bitten her and infected her with love-madness and left her a "dead" woman in Chinese society.

20

Chinese Medicine

I learned about love from my parents. I learned that love was unstable as water, that fathers were heroes one day, taking you out to feast at restaurants or to the beach on an unexpected Sunday; that the next day, they will disown you and call you an unbearable burden. I accepted that fathers were to be waited upon, hand and foot, at the brief twilight hour when they were home for their bath and dinner, before they left again "for business." It was an unquestioned rite in our house that we boiled hot water for our father's bath, placed his towel and fresh boxer shorts ready to his hand. It was our way of life that fathers had to be catered to and pampered, for they were the earners of wages. I learned early that fathers had temper tantrums, that they smashed and broke things if they did not get their way, that they threatened to leave the family, something that mothers never do.

Mothers were the opposite of fathers: they were dull as walls and furniture. They nagged, they disciplined, they had a moral or proverb for every occasion. If I complained as a child about something being "not fair," she'd say, "*Hak gau dau sek, baak gau dong joi.* The black dog steals the food, the white dog gets punished." (The world is not always fair or just.)

"*Choi kar m'chip hak, chut lo mo kwai yan.* Refusing to receive guests at home, on the road, no hosts or patrons." (Do unto others as you would have them do unto you.)

On prudence and saving for a rainy day, she gave us this proverb: "*Sek gai daan, m'sek gai na.* Eat the eggs but not the mother hen."

She had worldly wisdom: "*San don yau chek shi, sai kai mo chek yan.* In the forest, there are straight trees; in the world, there are no straight persons." Do not be too trusting—*tai ngan sik yan.* Wear eyes when meeting people. On the other hand, we were to be sensitive to others' needs, and not to be *dhin dhang dham,* an electric lightbulb staying brightly lit when lovers wanted to be alone in the dark.

My mother had proverbs for love, too. Often, on seeing lovers hand in hand in the public gardens, she would shake her head and say with a tolerant smile, "*Yau ching yam seui baau.* With love, drinking water fills the belly." I think she envied the euphoric time when lovers think they can be happy with love alone, though she'd warn us it was most unrealistic. One cannot live on love alone, echoing the English proverb "When poverty knocks at the door, love flies out the window."

My mother believed that one must make allowances, especially in a marriage. Since one was not perfect, one could not expect perfection or perfect happiness. She used to say, "*Daan ngan lou tai louh poh, yat ngan hoi, yat ngan mai.* The one-eyed man viewing his wife." (He keeps one eye blind to her faults.) She urged her children to study hard, for that was our only road out of poverty, a landscape she had grown too familiar with since her marriage. She stressed the need for a career, our own earning power, especially for us girls; she wanted us to avoid her fate, being chained to a loveless marriage, having to suffer a feckless husband. "Never stay with a man who hits you. The moment he lays a hand on you, you walk out the door. Or you are not my daughter."

My father never hit my mother, not because he did not want to. In some of their altercations, I have seen him poised with raised hand and voice to strike her. But he was prevented by her courage and reactions. She never flinched or cowered from him. She always grabbed a weapon, once a ceramic vase, once a large pair of scissors, and promised him she would harm him, she would spill his blood and his life, if he touched her. He believed her and shunted his violence aside, smashing many radios, gramophone records, once his brand-new TV set.

Until my early teen years, I believed they fought about money. I was not aware there were other conflicts underlying the fight over housekeeping money. When I was thirteen, my mother made me her confidante and shared with me her hopes and her betrayals. It was my stumbling accidentally onto one of the betrayals that thrust me into the role of secret sharer, and later, fierce champion that has been mine ever since.

I was thirteen the year I discovered there were dark secrets underlying the calm and easy rhythms of our very ordinary lives. I think this eventually led to my need to become a writer, to fill out the shapes and shadows beneath the surfaces people present to the world.

At thirteen, I wanted things and people to be what they seemed. Change bothered me. My body bothered me. It was changing, filling out. I was suddenly growing hair in strange places. My secret fear then was that I was changing into a beast, like Kafka's cockroach man. I asked my brother and he told me, from his vast experience of having lived two years more, that it was a natural thing; that even our parents had armpit and pubic hair.

Wanting confirmation, I asked Mother and she explained that I was not turning into an animal, just into a woman. She showed me how to crumple and pulverize cheap rice-chaff paper into coarse feminine napkins to catch the blood my body would begin to expel every month. She said rich women used soft, absorbent cotton napkins, Modess, instead of hard rice-chaff. I had naïvely assumed from the "Because . . ." ads that the elegant ladies were modeling dresses for that brand name.

I hated the physical process of becoming a woman. Month after month, I had "accidents" that mortified me, embarrassed me. It was made worse by the fact there would be no end to this process for the next forty years, an eternity to a teenager. At that time, a newspaper article brought me comfort. In Sweden, the first sex-change operations had been performed successfully. Though they were to change men into women, I felt cheered and confident that Western medicine would have achieved the ability to do the opposite operation by the time I grew up and saved enough money. I resolved to have my sex changed. This decision must have become embedded in my subconscious. Years later, when I was picking my baptismal name, I chose the uni-sexual name of Hilary.

Mother offered to let me have my hair permed. I think she

sensed my difficult adjustment to puberty. Most of my friends had
curly hair: the Malay girls came by theirs naturally, the Chinese girls
artificially. Mongolian straight black hair is a dominant genetic trait
and I had hair that stubbornly refused to curl, however much I
braided it. We all wanted curly hair and despised what we had.
Only when I came to America did I realize that our long, straight
black hair was a thing of beauty to Western eyes. I had begged
Mother for a permanent. She refused because we couldn't spare the
money. I knew her offer was her "handful of raisins," the sop she
used for getting us children to swallow bitter medicine.

In my experience, Chinese medicine always came in the form
of a huge bowl of bitter black broth with stomach-turning ingredi-
ents like earthworms, cockroaches, scorpions, creepy-crawly things,
fungi, and roots, simmered in a clay pot for hours to condense the
bitterness. One almost had to get well fast to avoid another dose of
the evil-smelling, evil-tasting liquid. Mother would give us a packet
of sweet golden raisins as a treat after, but the raisins never quite
erased the bitter aftertaste of the medicine.

My friend Swee Hoe recommended the Mei Wah Beauty Salon
on Kapar Road. It was located above the Bata Shoe Store in a row of
three-story shop-houses by the market. I climbed the stairs and
turned off the first landing. The stairs continued up to private apart-
ments above; I could tell by the shoes parked by the stairwell. In
Malaysia, you take off your shoes before entering a private home.

It was my first visit to a beauty salon and I was overwhelmed
by the smell. It was as if someone had washed the floor with *eau de
cologne* after a herd of cows had used the place as a bathroom. The
salon assaulted the eyes as well: bright pink walls, bright pink
linoleum floor, bright pink plastic seats, sinks, hair-dryers, rollers,
brushes. Contrast was provided by snippets of black hair on the
pink floor around each seat. The horror was amplified by mirror-
covered walls.

There were two customers, both their heads and faces hidden
by pink beehive hair-dryers and women's magazines. There were
two girls in pink smocks, both Chinese. One had dyed her hair red
and it looked most incongruous with her sallow complexion. The
other girl smiled and asked me in Cantonese how I wanted my hair
done. I showed her my pin-up of a magazine model, an English girl
whose beauty I yearned for, the high nose, the deep large green eyes,
the light brown hair; I hoped to achieve the look of her lustrous

curls. The salon girl shook her head, not unkind. She must have been used to customers coming in with unrealistic dreams. She said my hair was not long enough for that style. I picked one she suggested from her folder. She told me her name was Su-lin and started to pin and clip my hair. Then she shampooed it, rolled it in tight curlers, and drenched the curlers with pink perm solution (the source of the cow urine smell). She seated me under a steel contraption with a mass of dangling black wires, clamped a wire to each roller, handed me a bundle of magazines, and told me it would take thirty minutes for my hair to be "electrified." The Chinese word for perming is to "electrify the hair." I looked at my reflection in the mirror and decided I looked like Medusa in an extreme state of shock.

A long time later, or so it seemed to me as I sat in an odor of burning hair and ammonia, Su-lin released me, rinsed my hair (still in rollers), and stuck my head inside a pink beehive blow-dryer. I watched the other women taken out of their beehive captivity and their transformation as their rollers were removed and their hair fluffed out and styled. I began to read my magazines.

Looking up from an irritatingly arch article on "What Men Like in Women," I saw Father in the doorway. Actually, I saw his reflection in the mirror as I was sitting with my back to the door. I returned to my magazine and decided to let him surprise me when I had achieved my transformation.

I was happy he had come to take me home. At the time, my father outshone all the storybook heroes in my eyes. He played the saxophone (self-taught) in the local band; he was a lead actor in the Amateur Chinese Opera Association. He told magnificent stories and took me on outings with his large group of friends in their beautiful cars. He was a leader in the group even though his only means of transportation was a bicycle. He spent money freely and bought presents for me on those outings. His friends were as lighthearted and always game for adventure as he was.

I was disappointed when Su-lin finished my hair. Reality did not match my hopes. I was doubly disappointed when I looked for Father and he was not there. Su-lin said no one had come in after me.

I told Mother about the curious appearance and disappearance of Father at the Mei Wah Beauty Salon. She became very still for a moment, then she continued to spoon rice into my bowl. When I

pressed her for an explanation, she admitted that she had known for
five years that he kept a mistress above the Mei Wah.

I was not ready for such adult knowledge, though I must have
subconsciously picked up earlier hints so that her statement had the
force of truth, the click of the final piece in the jigsaw puzzle fitting
into place. I protested the impossibility of it, the unreason of it. I
tried to make my adults fit the rules of my then simpler universe.

"Is she more beautiful? What's she got that you haven't got?" I
couldn't understand my father's betrayal. Mother was beautiful by
Chinese standards: she still had a lovely figure. (Later she became
heavy after six pregnancies, too little exercise—housework drudgery
is not exercise; it does not burn calories—and too much starch in the
diet.) She waited on Father, trained us to wait on Father hand and
foot, and treated him as the most important person in the household
(except when they had their fights). She kept the house neat and
clean; she did not waste his money. What more, I argued, childish in
my fear of change and loss, could a man want?

Mother showed me a photograph of Father's Badminton Club.
Badminton is a serious sport in Malaysia. For us, the International
Thomas Cup is as big a deal as the World Cup in England or the
Superbowl in America. I'm still rather proud that I played for the
varsity team in my first year in college. Whether we won or lost the
season is a total fog to me. Strange, thinking back on it now. But I've
realized and grown to accept this fact about myself: I am not a fierce-
ly competitive person. I want to excel, to do well, to make the grade.
But I am content at that level; it does not bother me that I am not the
best; it does not bother me that there are others above me (as long as
the number is not too many). I think this habit of being content was
drilled into me by Mother's favorite proverb, "*San ko wan yow yat san
ko.* Tall mountain, there's another mountain taller." (Do not be arro-
gant: you may be the best here, but somewhere, there is someone
better than you.)

When Mother pointed out a woman in the Badminton Club
photograph as my father's mistress living above the Mei Wah
Beauty Salon, I stared. The woman was plain. She had a square face
and a square body. Her eyebrows were bushy, her eyes too small,
and her mouth too large.

"She's ugly. How can he prefer her to you?"

My mother must have asked herself this question many times.
And worked her way to a painful, partially correct answer. "Men

like change. Men like admiration. They need admiration and will choose it over devotion and a good housekeeper every time."

"You admire Father," I said. It seemed as obvious as mentioning that the sky was blue.

Her answer shocked me.

"I stopped admiring your father years ago. When Second Daughter died. When she was sick and he did not care enough to come home to take her to the doctor. It's hard to admire a selfish man who takes food from his children's mouths to take other women out for dinner. All these years, week in and week out, I am begging him for housekeeping money. Each time I beg, another piece of my heart turns to stone."

Years later, I would realize how this constant feeling of powerlessness in her life had embittered her. She was a woman whose intelligence, passion, and perceptions knew little outlet except secondhand, through her children. Surrounded by children and neighbors and relatives, my mother was essentially alone. She had to maintain the façade of a happy household to save the "face" of my father, of our family. My mother had a strong sense of integrity, of dignity. Until she turned to me as a receptive listener, there had been no one with whom she could share her hurt and shame at having an unsatisfactory husband; no one with whom she could speak the truth and not "lose face."

I sat while my rice grew cold and hard. I felt betrayed by both parents. My father in betraying my mother had betrayed me. I felt honored by my mother's telling me adult secrets. Yet the feeling was tinged with resentment. I felt burdened, weighed down, legs trembling like a colt carrying an overfed man. Looking back, I can name the thing I subconsciously grasped at the time. She made me grow up before I was ready.

"I would not stay after such betrayal," I said, quick to judge her. Thirteen is not an ideal confidante. At thirteen, there is only black and white, no varying shades of gray and compromise. Mother showed me a little of women's realities in 1959. Divorce was a social disgrace and rare. It was available for men whose wives cuckolded them, but few men wanted to "lose face" in such a drastic way. It was the social norm for men to have more than one woman. My father's lack of money was the only bar to his having concubines. A woman with little education and no children could become a house servant at subsistence pay. A woman who left her husband

and children for such a position would be vulnerable to unwanted male attentions; she would have a full belly but she would have "no face" to meet the eyes of the world. My mother explained that she could not abandon us children to the hardships a second wife would inflict on us; she could not earn enough to take us with her. Women who were dependant on their husbands had to shut their eyes (and mouths) to things like mistresses. My mother was progressive in her outlook. She believed fervently that times were changing. She was determined on equality for her daughters—we were to have as much education as we could attain. She knew daughters needed it more. She had sworn her daughters would not suffer as she had to.

I had never thought much about Mother—she was just there, like the roof over our heads. She sheltered, she scolded when we were out of line, she controlled our lives. It jarred me to learn she was powerless in a man's world. Compared to Father, who could come and go as he pleased, love whom and where and when he pleased, she was like a household pet constricted by invisible fences, her power real only to her children and her pots and pans.

In my own marriage, I have had a tiny taste of her lifelong powerlessness and the rage that seeps up with being caged. After the birth of our daughters, I stopped working to stay home full-time. It was my choice to be with my babies, yet I had an underlying uneasiness at having no income, no career of my own. One day, I purchased a trash compactor to reduce the bags of trash I had to haul to the curb each Tuesday night. My husband was shocked at the price: three hundred dollars for an unnecessary luxury. He felt I should have asked his permission (which he would have refused) before buying the contraption. He said that in future, I was not to buy anything over two hundred dollars without his okay. My mother had sensitized me. I recognized the male power play: first, to demean what I did in our household as of little worth, not meriting a labor-saving device. My husband did not subscribe to the macho myth that the "Man of the House" takes out the trash. In this and many practical aspects, ours is a very Asian household. The second part of the power play demoted me from equal to subordinate, from spouse to child, someone who needed to ask permission before action. My reaction was to demand that he pay me a salary (retroactive, please) at the going rate for full-time housekeepers. "Fair's fair," I said, "if you are going to treat me like an underling, then I want my underling's pay to call my own; money I can use to buy trash, much less trash compactors, if I so desire." In fairness to my husband, he was not consciously seeking to belittle me or reduce my self-worth. He was thinking of being prudent with money, saving for the children's college educations. But if I had acceded to his restrictive proposition, my sense of self-worth would have been eroded and we would have stepped onto the slippery slope of resentment, of feeling betrayed and unloved, that is the beginning of the breakdown of many marriages. I have to thank my mother for the lessons she taught me, consciously and unconsciously.

That was the only time I had my hair permed. I decided I preferred having straight hair. I also gave up the idea of changing myself into a man. I stopped liking raisins; I was a grown woman, and could take my Chinese medicine in all its bitterness.

Father

1

It was better than carnival day to see
you, the heroine in the opera, slender
in a gown of sequined silk, diamond
pins in your elaborate wig, your hands
arcing in grace-lineated gestures
as your voice stroked and stretched,
fish glistening upstream
against the roaring of cymbals.

Older, your waist thickened,
you played the hero, strode high
over invisible doorsills, rode unseen horses,
made invisible cities fall
with serpentine ripplings of flags while drums
pounded through my ears and my blood.
Later, you played the saxophone in the band.
I knew you could do anything.

2

My first memory is you, playing
with me and Sister who died.
You sloped a plywood board,
conjured Monte Carlo's Grand Prix
for our little lead cars.
You were commentator and sound effects
and we were squeals and admiration.

3

Those were rain days in our growing season,
and rare. You sowed and followed
the freedom of butterflies, abandoned us
for flights with beautiful women.
Returning for the harvest, you are surprised
there are blackbirds in your ricefield.

—from *Paper Boats*

21

Earth Dragon, Metal Monkey

I knew early that I was a Fire Dog and that Brother was a Wood Monkey. Mother told us our zodiac signs though she kept our times of birth secret, in case an ill-wisher obtained the vital information from our careless mouths and caused us harm. Mother still has this phobia about ill-wishers.

Once, she was very afraid Father's current mistress would find a *bomoh*, a witch-doctor, to put a hex on her. She'd heard that the mistress had had two abortions and was desperate to be accepted as a secondary wife into our family. This could not happen until Mother agreed to accept her. Father kept dropping hints about how helpful Mother would find having another woman in the house. "Not at all," Mother said, calmly, each time he brought up the subject. "Another woman wouldn't be helpful as she would be a dead woman the instant you bring her across my doorsill. I will kill her myself."

Though she hid it well from Father, Mother was really afraid that she might be hexed into accepting the ceremonial cup of tea from the woman and be stuck forever with a concubine. Or worse, be hexed into illness and dying, leaving us to the indifferent care of Father and a new wife. She became obsessive about burning her fingernail parings and hairs from her comb so that no one could use them to bewitch her. One afternoon, she came home and furtively showed me a small yellow silk pouch tied with red thread.

"What is it?" I asked.

"The dried phallus of an all-black dog without a single white hair on it. It's very rare and costs a lot of money."

"What's it for?"

"It's an amulet. It'll protect me from all ill wishes and any kind of magic."

Mother hid the amulet somewhere in her bedroom and stopped worrying about Father's mistress. I had my doubts about the authenticity of the amulet but did not voice them. I was happy Mother was back to normal again.

There are twelve Chinese zodiac signs, under the influence of twelve different animals, each to a year. They are: Rat, Ox, Tiger, Rabbit, Dragon, Snake, Horse, Sheep, Monkey, Rooster, Dog, and Pig, in the order that these animals came to pay their respects to the Lord Buddha when he was dying (or transiting to Nirvana) under his *Boh* tree. The strongest and most auspicious sign is the Dragon. My mother was born in the year of the Dragon and she claims this was probably why she survived, unlike the five siblings who preceded her and who died in infancy. Her maternal grandmother named her TuckKhoon (Achieving Power) at her birth, but her parents called her by a less awesome everyday-use name, LinTei (Little Lotus). When she turned sixty, Mother changed her name from TuckKhoon (Achieving Power) to TuckKhoon (Achieving Perception) by changing the character for *Khoon*. The name sounded the same but the meaning was more expressive of her hopes, her self-image, she said.

She had been a desperately wanted child, and when a baby brother was born later, her parents felt that it was her luck that had brought him to them; she was their bright star, the north star, in their child-dark sky. The first and longest certainty of her childhood, she knew, was her father's love for her.

I had adored my grandfather and was shocked to hear Mother say, "He was a wife-beater," as she reminisced about her childhood. "He used to slap my mother around whenever he got angry—she was afraid of him. Once a man starts hitting his wife, it's very hard for him to stop. It becomes a habit. That's why I never let your father lay a hand on me."

I remembered many nights huddling under the kitchen table with Brother LeeLang while my parents screamed and hurled sharp-edged words at each other, remembered times when my father moved toward her with his hand raised in a fist, how she would snatch up anything within reach, a pair of sewing scissors, a glass vase, a broom, and face him: "You hit me and you'll pay with your blood!" We could tell that our normally gentle mother meant what she said; she would be more vicious than he if he used physical violence. Father saw it too. Instead of smashing his fist into her face, he smashed it into her framed photograph or his radio, something that broke with noise and fragments. Once, he broke all his favorite gramophone records. Later, when they owned a television, he smashed it with an iron pipe. But he did not hit her, though he wanted to during some of their fights.

Father was born in the year of the Metal Monkey, a fun-loving sign, and he has all the wily charm and salesmanship of that sign. Unfortunately, he married an Earth Dragon, a straightforward "iron-hand without velvet glove" autocrat, who did not appreciate his sleight-of-hand tricks and refused to admire his cleverness when he failed to be a responsible husband. He turned to more congenial company away from the house, and she grew more bitter toward him. Their worst fight was when she had to have his pay garnished for our upkeep.

"It is a wife's duty to protect a husband's back. She put a knife in it," Father said. "When I had a fight with the boss's son, she apologized to him instead of asking me for my side of the story."

"You were fighting over a woman," Mother said flatly. "I got you your job back."

"All you care about is money! I can get any job I want; I don't need you groveling to my relatives for my job."

Father did find himself a new job. With another uncle. Later, he went into business for himself with money borrowed from a cousin. He made money easily. He also spent with ease. And in the end, he had empty pockets, an empty cash-box, and Mother had to repay the cousin's loan with her savings from housekeeping money.

The biggest difference between my parents was that Mother, dragon-like, always had a hoard, a little savings put by and could make money appear for a needy day. Father had magic, too. He could make money disappear. True to his Monkey sign, he treated money like fresh fruit, to be consumed on the spot. Their fights occurred when Father needed cash for some venture or fun or other

My parents on a bridge, midway in their marriage

disappearing trick and Mother refused to lend him any from her hoard.

Mother said her father stopped beating her mother when she was a toddler. Whenever he started raising his voice at her mother, she would run to him with outstretched arms. He would automatically pick her up and cuddle her, which tied up his hands until his rage was past. She knew, even at the age of one, that she could do this with impunity, knowing he loved her above any rage or unreason. My brother and I never had the confidence to interpose our small bodies between our father's wrath and its target. We dared only to raise our scared voices, begging him: "Please, do not be angry with Mother." Somehow, we knew, we were not large enough in our father's affections to shield our mother when the rage was on him.

22

The Joyful Vanguards

My thirteenth year, I was obsessed by the Kelang River. For weeks, I plotted and schemed and rejected one plan after another to get my parents to let me cross it on my own, to let me ride my bicycle to school. I could not articulate why this was so terribly important, at the time. But I knew that if I could just obtain this small freedom, I could reach out for more, yet undreamed of, freedoms.

The Convent of the Holy Infant Jesus Girls' School, which I attended, was in South Kelang, separated from my home in North Kelang by a distance of three miles which included the river. The Kelang River was a mile wide at this point as it opened itself to join the sea. The river water rose and fell, six to eight feet, twice a day with the tides. Passage across the broad brown water was achieved by jolting and bumping across a pair of temporary pontoon bridges. Built by Japanese troops during the Second World War, the bridges were actually continuous rafts of huge logs lashed together and kept afloat by empty metal cylinders under them. The pontoon bridges rose and fell steeply with the tides. They had flimsy rope railings to mark their edges. By age thirteen, I was allowed the freedom of riding my bicycle in North Kelang. I was not allowed to cross the river. I had to ride the school bus back and forth.

This meant I had to come home immediately after regular school hours. I desperately wanted permission to cross the river on my own. There were extracurricular activities—badminton tournaments, net-ball games, field and track events. I was athletic and wanted to compete in the afterschool sports events. I did eventually take many prizes and still have the tiny silver cups I received, with such pride, at the time. But my most urgent reason for freedom was the Joyful Vanguards Club.

The Joyful Vanguards was a Catholic clone of the Girl Scouts of America. It was led by Miss Goh, our enthusiastic history teacher, who had just come back to Malaysia from teacher training in England. All my South Kelang schoolmates joined and raved about the fun and camaraderie at their meetings. For weeks I tried to wheedle permission to cross the river on my own, without success. One morning, I found an excuse—a forgotten homework assignment. I rode a friend's bicycle home from school to fetch it. Father followed me on his bicycle back to school. This demonstration of ability had the desired result. Father conceded I could manage the pontoon bridges and I joined the Joyful Vanguards.

This new mobility opened the door to another important freedom. I joined the Kelang Library near the school, paying its monthly fees with my lunch money. With the books I borrowed, I roamed the world, past, present, and future. I read *Gone with the Wind, Dracula, World Fairy Tales.* I read Poe, Emily Dickinson, the Brontë sisters; gobbled up Georgette Heyer, Jane Austen, George Eliot, Barbara Cartland, Agatha Christie, Charles Dickens—I read them all and did not care that one was good writing and one was pulp.

The library sated another hunger I had not even known I possessed. To learn my cultural identity. I read everything I could find on the Chinese—Arthur Waley's Chinese poets, the *Analects*, the *Tao Te Ching*, Chinese fairy tales, and classics in translation like *The Three Kingdoms, Dream of the Red Chamber, The Water Margin.* I borrowed Lin Yutang's books, Han Su-yin's books, Robert Van Gulik's Judge Dee mysteries, Fairbanks and Reischauer's histories of China, again and again. Later, when I was in college at the University of Malaya and had a little money to spare from my Malaysian government scholarship, I saw Chinese movies assiduously.

Looking back, I realized the river divided my mind as surely as it did my daily life. At home, I was a cog in a fixed social structure: eldest daughter in a poor family meant you cared for the babies, waited on your elders, did housework, did schoolwork, asked no questions, aired no opinions. The young were not supposed to think on their own. "When you have eaten as much rice as I have eaten salt, then you can have an opinion," our elders used to say, each time we spoke out of turn. At extended family gatherings, Mother reminded us children, we were "poor relations," and not to get into games or arguments with the children of the rich relatives. Rich meant right in our society.

At school, I could exercise a small amount of free will and make choices in the classes I took: Science track, Arts track, or Domestic Science track, which meant cooking and sewing. Everyone knew Domestic Science was for girls who'd get married and have babies right after they finished school. I opted for Science track as science teachers were always in demand and Mother had drummed into our heads, early, the need for job security. Though the colonial British system of education did not encourage creative thinking, the nuns did present us with radically different social structures. British and European history is studded with individuals and their achievements: Sir Stamford Raffles who founded Singapore, James Brooke who became the first white Rajah of Sarawak, and Napoleon Bonaparte. American history was skimped as it was a painful reminder of British failure. But we did get hints of recalcitrant colonials and pilgrims demanding freedom of worship.

The Joyful Vanguards had three-hour-long meetings once a week. There, we learned pledges of "decent, communal behavior" based on Christian concepts; we learned that poor and rich were considered equal by the Western God—"It is harder for a rich man to enter Heaven than for a camel to pass through a needle's eye," claimed the Christian Gospel. We were given permission to play, to have friends, to have fun. This was a bold departure from all that we had learned. As proper Asians, we had been programmed to behave like miniature adults; we did not "play" in our cultural environment. Suddenly, the world did not have to be all browns and white, it was permissible to have color, music, change. The white overlords of our country allowed it, approved it. Suddenly, rich relatives were no longer the highest authority in my life. I rejected my mother's pantheon of teachers, rich elderly female relatives, especially after I found that her chief guru, Grand-Aunt One, could be completely wrong in her wisdom.

Mother had been worried about what a clumsy child I was. I had dropped and cracked three rice bowls one month, washing up after dinner. She consulted her best authority, rich Grand-Aunt One. Grand-Aunt One told her that I was shamming clumsiness to get out

of doing chores. Mother came home, yanked my head out of the
book it was in, and walloped me with a rattan cane for such devi-
ousness, deceit, and laziness. She declared that I must have learned
such wicked "Western people ways" from the Joyful Vanguards. She
threatened to stop letting me attend meetings. If she had beaten me
for being careless, clumsy, I would not have minded. I was used to
beatings; I was often beaten for my lack of respect for Chinese codes
of behavior, for arguing, for asking stupid, impertinent questions. I
got extra lashes of the rattan for protesting that Grand-Aunt was
wrong about me.

My older brother tried to console me. "Look, it's stupid to try
to reason with grown-ups. You'll only get beaten more. Be patient
like me. Wait. Wait until you have money and the power. Then, you
can tell them they were wrong." I looked at LeeLang in surprise. I
thought he really believed our traditions. "You mean you don't
always agree with Mother?" He said, "I disagree plenty but I never
say it out loud. I keep my thoughts safely in my head. Then I don't
get beaten for them." I thought he was not very honest but accepted
that his advice was well-meant. I was grateful that he had revealed
his real self to me, albeit secretly and without risk. I was comforted
to know I was not alone in my outcast state.

Later that night, as I lay aching on my mat, I figured out why
this caning had hurt so much more than others. It was the injustice
of it. Honor, kindness, and integrity were concepts I had picked,
after much thought, to be the foundations of my self, the person I
wanted to face in the mirror, the rest of my life. That this honest,
honorable person I was trying so hard to become was not readily
apparent to my usually perceptive mother came as a shock to me.
What I thought of as attempts to communicate, to achieve better
understanding with her, my mother saw as rebellion, rejection of her
cultural values, and threats to overthrow her authority. Thanks to
Grand-Aunt One, I had been wrongly accused, judged, sentenced,
and punished without even a hearing. That night, I swept all the
statues of rich relatives off my mental altar. I also dropped all the
Chinese gods who needed to be bribed for favors. And I acknowledged that my mother was human and could err.

Mother was right in one of her accusations. I was learning
"Western people ways" in the Joyful Vanguards. I was absorbing
radical ideas antithetical to Chinese canon from the innocent songs
we sang for pleasure and group bonding; songs mostly of American

origin, though we did not know it at the time. We picked up ideas of freedom of expression: "If you're happy and you know it, clap your hands . . ."; hedonism: "Kookaburra"; loyalty and friendship; cooperation: "Danny Boy," "Michael, Row the Boat Ashore"; the evils of oppression: "Old Black Joe," "Old Folks at Home"; the acceptance of justice, hope, and the right to struggle. We sang "On Top of Spaghetti" and "Yankee Doodle Dandy," and learned that humor was not necessarily disrespectful or bad. We began to think about mortality and the transience of life outside the fixed, fatalistic wheel of Chinese faith: "All My Trials," with the line "If religion were a thing money could buy, then the rich would live and the poor would die," reinforced my seedling rebellion against my people's cultural values, where physical striving for material wealth and eating well seemed to be the main principles for living.

I did not know I was becoming a cultural renegade. I only knew I felt meaningful, alive, and happy at Joyful Vanguards meetings, whether we worked on learning the joy of giving with a "Help the Poor" project or made ceramic ashtrays for our fathers, regardless of whether they smoked or not. My father smoked, so his pleasure at receiving my lumpy, crude ashtray was as great as mine in the giving.

I did not realize the extent of the impoverishment in my mother's mental life until I visited home recently. She was most excited at a line she had heard from the pastor of our neighbor's church. "All the world's a stage, and all its men and women merely players. This life is only a drama, soon over." "If I had known this way of looking at things before, I would not have felt so trapped all my life!" she said. My English teachers had taught me Shakespeare's immortal metaphor when I was fourteen. My mother did not have this wonderful perspective presented to her until she was sixty-seven! How different her life might have been, had she, and my father, had the same opportunities I did.

My father had wanted his children to be educated in Chinese at the parochial schools. Mother had insisted on English education for us, so that we could have better work opportunities in a British-colonized country. She did not know she was cutting me loose from the millstone of Chinese materialism, that she was giving me the greatest gift, after the gift of life: freedom to walk into non-Chinese worlds from which I would bring back ideas and a language with which I could invent myself.

23

The House
on Palace Road

The lane we lived on was actually a packed laterite excuse of a lane, with wild grass tufts dividing two groves of bare dirt made by feet, bicycles, motorbikes, and an occasional car or lorry. Malaysian earth is poor soil, leached by 100 inches of annual rainfall to a raw red color, stripped of nutrients, and baked to a tired orange by the tropical sun at 90 plus degrees daily. Outside the front door of each house was a plywood rack for shelving shoes as we went barefoot indoors. Mother would move the rack of shoes inside last thing at night before locking up, in case someone should steal our shoes. I pointed out to her once that they were worn, sorry-looking shoes and I didn't think any thief would stoop to steal them. She said it did not matter; who knew what a thief would stoop to. The main thing was that we were too poor to replace our shoes and therefore could not take the risk.

I never knew if other families locked up their shoes at night. I knew they took them off before going inside. My Indian friends, who lived in houses similar to ours, shook off their footwear at their door. My Malay friends, who lived in lovely breezy houses of brown wood raised on stilts, took off their slippers and shoes at the bottom of their wooden stairs before climbing the eight feet up to their homes. I thought everyone went barefooted indoors as this was true of all the houses I knew, until I was fifteen. That year I met Susan L., a Eurasian girl, and began to visit her Western-style home. On my first visit, I had my right shoe off when she said, "Keep your shoes on," and led the way into her house. I hobbled after her, stuffing my foot back into its shoe, my mouth falling open as I saw the spacious rooms and furniture that she took for granted and passed without a glance.

My friend Susan had eminent parents. They were on our school's Board of Governors. Susan came to school in a big white car driven by Hashim, the chauffeur. All the girls (we were all poor) were in awe of her. Though friendly to her in school, no one ever ventured up Jalan Istana (Palace Road) to call on her. Her mother was physician to the Royal House of Selangor and everyone in town knew her as "the English woman doctor." If one needed a second opinion on a medical matter, one went, as a matter of course, to "the English woman doctor." She looked English, with reddish-brown hair, blue eyes, and fair skin. Her practice had the mystique of English blood, English training, and English power, though the British Empire was in its decline. Susan's father was a publisher and printer. Both parents were of Anglo-Indian descent.

The first time I bicycled uphill on Palace Road in the hot sun, I asked myself what I was doing there, out of place, out of breath, out of handkerchiefs to wipe my sweating face. I had one good reason to visit: I thought my friend Susan was lonely for company. There were reasons not to visit: I was poor, she was rich. Poor people should not encroach on the rich. My friends would call me "pigeon-eyed," a sycophant. My thoughts ran back and forth as I pedaled. I was not a dog, to fawn on the rich; I was not a snob, so impressed by wealth I must reject a rich friend to prove otherwise. I liked Susan; I liked talking to her. She had interesting things to say. Since she was carried off in the white car immediately after school back to her castle, I would have to storm the castle and any adjunct moats and dragons to continue the friendship, I told myself bravely. Besides, Susan had said, "Come and visit me. I'm always home after school." We all knew where she lived. The girls had gone as a group, once, to visit the princess in her tower.

I rode up to the huge bungalow-style brick house with half an acre of well-behaved grass and rare orchids. There was no moat, only a white circular drive and a gardener trimming bushes. There were no dragons, but there were two large dogs, almost as daunting. One was a Great Dane, huge as a water-buffalo calf with yellow eyes. The other was an English mastiff, with jowled cheeks and frowning eyes. The Great Dane leaped up and down and ran around me and my bicycle, its maw opened wide to emit deep-chested barks. The mastiff growled a low menacing vibrato. I kept my bicycle between me and the dogs as best as I could. Luckily, the loud barking brought a pink-cheeked, white-haired Santa Claus lady in a print housedress to my rescue. "Down, Ular, shut up. Go away, scoot, you dogs, do. Hello, I'm Nana. Who are you?"

Keeping a wary eye on the dogs, who were now wagging their tails and trying, unsuccessfully, to look harmless, I said my name and why I was there. "How lovely. Yoohoo, Susan, you've got a visitor!" At which point I began to take off my shoes and Susan stopped me and led me to her room. Her room was half the size of my house!

Susan's house had four bathrooms! Each was the size of the bedroom I shared with my siblings. They had flush toilets and color-coordinated bathtubs. I thought of home, where we shared one outhouse with our neighbors. Home, where we had been so elated to have a smooth cement floor. All the rooms in Susan's house had rugs, lush thick velvety rugs on polished wood floors. The living room had a piano, upholstered chairs, and sofas. And an expanse of space around each item. I had never seen so much space to spare in a home before. There was a Chinese house servant to keep everything shining and dust-free.

Susan's room had white sheepskin rugs, and the thing I envied most, shelves and shelves of books. Even a complete set of *Encyclopedia Britannica* in tooled maroon leather. She had her own record player and we listened to her favorite music, my first encounter with Rodgers and Hammerstein musicals. We talked about things familiar: school, the nuns, classes. And things new to me: the kings of England (she had shelves of Churchill's histories, the Plantagenet kings), Richard III in Shakespeare and real history. We discussed American musicals—the characters and plots of "Oklahoma," "South Pacific." Susan lent me books, wanted to share her love of Dickens, Austen. In her quiet way, without words, she let me know she was glad I had come and would be glad if I came again.

Nana, Mrs. Santa Claus, was Susan's maternal grandmother. Nana came in, light on her feet, light in her hair, smiling. She brought fresh-squeezed lemonade and cookies. She showed me the family album, Susan's baby pictures, said over and over how delighted she was to know Susan's friend. My grandmother glowered silently at visitors. I loved Nana from the day we met.

On my third visit, the English mastiff bit me. It had begun to rain as I reached the driveway. I thought the dogs had gotten used to me by then. Ular, the Great Dane, had stopped barking at me. I rode up to the front door and jumped off my bike. A silent mass of muscle, fur, and teeth crashed into my side and sank sharp teeth into my thigh. I don't remember if I screamed. I must have made some noise, for suddenly Nana was there, beating at the dog, tugging open its jaw, scolding it, and assuring me alternately: "Stupid dog, let go. Don't worry, he's had his shots. Open up, you fool! I've got iodine. You must be hurting. Poor baby. It's the pound for you next, you brainless mutt! Don't you know Butch is a friend?"

Susan and her family always called me "Butch," short for "Butcher," which was Susan's nickname for me. Being in different grades and classes, we had become friends over an incident at school. As Fifth Form (Senior) class monitor, I had the task of obtaining dissection animals for the joint Fourth (Junior) and Fifth Form science class. Usually, this went routinely. I bought the frogs, rabbits, and mice from local families cheaply (or the pet shop, which cost more) and brought them to school on the appointed day. On the day appointed for the dissection of the guinea pig, Miss Vatchelu, the science teacher, fell sick. A week later, when she had recovered, the guinea pig had acquired a name and become a pet of the class. Susan was a leader of the "Save Horace, the Guinea Pig!" movement and pleaded with me to buy another guinea pig for sacrifice to science and Miss Vatchelu. I had to refuse, having no spare funds for such a thing. I acquired the nickname of "Butcher," shortened to "Butch," to show the girls still liked me. And I acquired a new friend. In our time of innocence, no one thought of the lesbian connotations of my nickname. I only learned of them years later.

In spite of the attack by the dog, I became a frequent visitor at the house on Palace Road. We spent many afternoons in Susan's room, listening to music, talking about novels, plots, life, quoting favorite poets to each other. Shakespeare, Wordsworth, Tennyson, Emily Dickinson, Yeats kept us company. And always, Nana would come after an hour or two, with cookies and lemonade and stories and songs of her girlhood in India, stories about her Irish father and Indian mother. Sometimes, Nana would dance an Irish jig for me.

Susan would say, "Now, Nana," and look a little embarrassed at her grandmother's exuberance. She need not have worried. Nana amazed me, delighted me, constantly. She was so different from the grandmothers I knew. I had thought grandmothers soured in old age. They always wore somber colors and disapproved of laughter and young people. Nana showed me that old age was what you made of it. She wore bright print housedresses, splashed eau-de-cologne on herself and me, "keeps us cool and makes us smell nice." She laughed about growing old. "I shouldn't have let my arms grow flabby, like banners. It's a terrible thing! When I wave, my arm waves back at me. On the other hand, I'm a walking gymnasium for myself. My left arm has a punching bag for my right and vice versa. See? Bop bop boppity bop."

Susan's parents, when I met them, turned out to be kind and hospitable, often inviting me to stay over for meals and several times to the movies in Kuala Lumpur with them. On such evenings, Mr. L. would drive me and my bicycle home to ask permission for the outing. I learned to eat with a knife and fork at Susan's house. I learned that mealtimes were for conversation as well as food. In their house, I entered another world, a far far different world from the one I inhabited daily; a world where the young were allowed, invited to speak their thoughts, where what they said was heard with consideration by their elders. I was always a little shocked when Dr. L. would ask me what I thought about the topic under discussion. I began to think. I began to examine the information in my head, to question aspects of the knowledge I had always accepted passively and to allow myself to arrive at judgment for myself, so that the next time Dr. L. or Nana asked me for an opinion, I would have one, not mumble into my napkin or turn to Susan for help, like a trapped guinea pig.

My Father's Orchids Are Beautiful

My father drives miles
out of town to buy bud-grafts,
spindley parasite plants
waving blind roots in the air.
He haggles with men missing
toes, fingers, buys more
from a woman lacking a nose—
there is no shrinking in him
from these cured lepers; he admires
their touch with orchids.

My father does not care
that his friends are false,
that his many lovers have forgotten.
Each morning, he swallows pills
for diabetes and blood pressure,
spills his urine into a glass tube
to read the barometer for living.
He mixes charcoal and earth,
chips of broken clay pots
for the purples and mauves,
adds cow manure for pinks and whites.
"Spider orchids are weeds," he says,
"Unchecked, they kill the beautiful ones."

My father tolerates the Chinese gods
my mother brings home to prevent demons.
He likes Jesus and Buddha, has read
the Koran; shrugs at the promise
of belly dancers in a dead tomorrow.
"All roads lead to Death, a country of dry bones,
nothing to do or see there. Fools
postpone pleasure for a possibility."

—from *Tigerbone Wine*

24

Chinese New Year

My favorite holiday was Chinese New Year. Each time, I was wakened by the rat-a-tat-tat of firecrackers and the ko-koo-ko-roo of startled roosters. I would towel the sweat from my face, knowing it was going to be another scorching Malaysian day. But today nobody minded the heat. Today was the first day of the Chinese New Year. It always began with the loud explosions of firecrackers to scare away evil spirits. Everyone wanted a full day of sunshine and clear skies to herald an auspicious year.

For a month, Mother had been busy preparing the house, and us, for the new year. She had scrubbed floors, cleaned the altar gods and made new clothes for us to wear, bought new inscriptions of the names of the two door gods and pasted them on the front door. Wealthier Chinese houses had colorful pictures of the door gods on their doors. With us, their names, General Ch'in Ch'uing and General Yu-Chih Ching Teh, on red paper strips, were just as efficacious and would keep demons and devils away from our house, Mother said.

"How did the two generals become door gods?" I asked. Mother was grinding shrimp to make shrimp chips, her New Year specialty. She said, "Emperor Tai Tsung was plagued by demons during his reign. Every night, demons came and pinched his nose and toes. They bit him all over and caused him such pain, he dared not close his eyes. When they learned of his problem, his two brave

141

generals offered to stand guard outside his bedroom door all night long, which they did for a week. That week, the emperor slept as peacefully as a drunken immortal. But his generals got red-eyed and green-faced from lack of sleep. The clever emperor decided to have their pictures painted and pasted on his bedroom doors, in hopes they would fool the demons. This worked so well, everyone decided to use the generals to guard their houses too."

The week before New Year, Mother would remind us, again and again, of things we must not do on New Year's Day. We were not to use brooms, dustpans, or feather dusters, or throw anything out of the house. Gathering and throwing away dust was like throwing away the new year's luck. For the first fifteen days of the new year, we were not to think or say inauspicious words like "wreaths," "death," or other words associated with funerals, sickness, and bad luck. We knew we would eat rich meats, waxed duck, sweet pork sausages, and roast chicken, with our rice during the fifteen days. We never ate porridge at the new year. Porridge, watery rice, would bring wet weather throughout the year. Sewing and needlework were not permitted in case blood be drawn. We knew our parents would not scold or beat us for anything, however naughty we were, lest scolding became the pattern for the year. The one restriction I had trouble obeying was the rule about not washing my hair during the first five days of the new year, in case I washed away our luck. I hated the feel of dirty hair.

Looking back, I am reminded of the child development book, *The Magic Years*. It put forth the thesis that the child believes he is a magician, creator of his world, believes he conjures up the world with magical thinking; that his parents "poof" into existence when his thought creates them. My natal culture seems to have a similar child-like conception of the denizens of their spirit world: gods, demons, and luck spirits.

A week before the New Year, Mother bought a tall sugarcane plant home and leaned it against the kitchen wall by the kitchen god's altar. She also bought New Year *queh,* a kind of sticky rice pudding steamed into a hard paste, with lots of sugar in it. The *queh* was to sweeten the Kitchen God's mouth when he climbed up the sugar cane to Heaven and made his annual report on our family's behavior. The red paper with his name and attributes was torn off and burned on the twenty-third evening of the twelfth month and replaced with a fresh new one on the last day of the year. My first doubts about the adequacies of Chinese gods were wakened by the Kitchen God. Somehow, a sugarcane ladder to Heaven and a weakness for sugar suggested humanity rather than godhead.

New Year, for me as a child, was always a time of excitement and anticipation. I'd wake up knowing "good things" would happen that day. My friends and I would meet, with our bicycles, and wheel through the town, a flock of common sparrows, transformed in our brand-new brightly colored dresses into kingfishers. We'd stop at the homes of everyone we knew, calling out *"Gong Si Fatt Chai! We wish you prosperity!"* (the traditional Chinese formula for a happy New Year). The women of the house would bring out their New Year specialties—nine-layered rice cakes, salted peanuts, candied ginger, shrimp chips, taro crabs, delicious melt-in-the-mouth "love-letter" (pirouettes) wafers. They'd offer us fizzy ginger ale or sarsaparilla. Carbonated drinks were a special treat; we never got them the rest of the year. At the end of the visit, they'd give us red packets of "luck money." As we wheeled our bikes away, we'd make them happy, calling out more wishes for prosperity for them.

For us kids, the main purpose of the day was the collecting of "luck money." Often, we'd stop under the generous shade of a saga tree to count our loot. Most of the mothers gave us 40 cents or 60 cents, always even numbers for luck and balance. We were all poor families. My friend Kim Choo's grandmother, who owned a furniture store, always gave me a dollar. I was her favorite of Kim Choo's friends. It took a lot of visits, and our voices grew a little hoarse by the end of the day with calling out prosperity wishes, before we accumulated the magnificent amount of $60 each. Which we generally did. I knew the money was not mine to keep. Brother and I each got to keep $5; we had to give most of our loot to Mother. If she did not have our help to replace the "luck money" she had been handing out, she would run short of housekeeping money and we would have Grandmother throwing tantrums, writhing on the floor, and howling at the gods, for sending her an evil daughter-in-law who made her eat plain rice and cheap vegetables with not a sliver of meat. As for Father, he would get on his bicycle and ride back to town to eat out if he saw there was no meat on the table.

The family altar with ancestral tablet
and Father's favorite chair below it

My Father and Terminal Kidney Failure

1

Six A.M. We arrive at the Dialysis Clinic.
The dark of pre-dawn. You get out of the car,
slow and careful, shuffle your way
across the lobby floor, an old man
on a slippery path, wary of falls.
You pull pale feet from your shoes,
the shoes Mother washed yesterday
after you stepped into dog droppings
on our way to the coffee-shop, your stride
brisk and careless, as you said, "*Koay Teoy*
with mussels and chili and bean-sprouts,
that's what I want for breakfast!"

In the clinic, you walk to a favorite chair,
stake your silent claim.
You stand there,
eyes unfocused, patient
like fog, and as persistent.
There are fake-leather easy chairs.
"Useless things," you say. "They get too hot."
You prefer the casual lounge chairs, with
happy colors of red, white, and blue, colors
of America, summer, sea, and sand.
Diverted from their original purpose, they
serve here on a silent beach
of anti-septic white tile.
In air-conditioned cool, their plastic will not
crack from wind and sun, they will not hear
the calls of sea-gulls or sand-castling children.
They will hear, not the singing of exuberant waves,
only the sad songs of tired blood.

2

You bare your left arm
and its specially vented veins for hook-up
to the machine that cleans your blood for you
in place of your failed kidneys. Your arms
are dark with sun and stippled with age.
You close your eyes, sleep away the hours
that you have to endure the ebb and flow
of your blood as it runs from your vein,
dark with toxins and body wastes, through coils
of clear plastic tubing into the machine and returns,
cleansed and bright red.
          For today's second breakfast,
you want baked taro with shrimp, soybean pudding.
I fetch it from the little market
and feed you. You doze some more, ignore
the chatter of the other patients
except to point out how dirty their blood
looks, compared to yours. I nod,
though all look the same to me.

You are the oldest patient here, you say
proudly, and dismiss the tragedy
of their younger lives. You have no interest
in other people's suffering, yours fills your mind.

There's a pretty Filipino in the lobby,
a housemaid waiting for her boyfriend,
a dialysis patient, her employer's brother.
"Stupid girl, wasting her time
seducing a sick man," you said.

I am grateful for your unkind words.
Hard-headed and hard-hearted,
they give me hardness.
Hardness I desperately need, to bear this.
To bear seeing you in the chair, your blood
so wrongly spindling outside your body.
To disclaim sorrow avoiding a name,

knowing that in two days, I have to
come again to see it all re-done
and real.

3

The doctor comes. You tell him you're fine.
All your life, you've lied to doctors,
treated their exams like tests you must pass,
by cheating if you have to. You complain
about symptoms, pain to laymen, your children,
your wife. We were always your messengers
of bad news to the emperor.

You recall times from childhood
when your mother left you, unfed, forgotten,
in busy shops of indifferent relatives;
how you went hungry from dawn to dark,
too timid to ask for food.
You boast about the speed with which
you could finish a meal before,
regret slowing down now.
You brood about food, dream of eating
juicy *Teo Chew* duck noodles with globules of fat,
crispy skin of roast suckling pig,
steamed farm chicken, white and tender,
stir-fried beef with spring onions.
Your blood pulses through the coils of tubing
and returns, brings luster to your eyes,
warmth to your toes.

Four hours later, you step out
with purpose in your eyes. You say,
"Let's go to the Coliseum Restaurant.
I feel like a good beef steak."

Chewing pink beef, you talk about the first time
you went to a smorgasbord, a buffet-style
"all you can eat" restaurant. You did not realize

you could have as many helpings as you wanted.
Later, you went back and made up for it.
I understand why you want to eat
every two hours. Your life is a buffet
with its closing time posted and
you want all the seconds you can get.

25

The Needs of the Dead

Kechil di-kandung ibu,
besar di-kandung adat, mati di-kandung tanah.

Small, man is enclosed by mother;
adult, by custom; dead, by earth.

—Malay Proverb

It was the day after my father's funeral. I was sitting in the kitchen, thinking that there was a comforting sense of closure about burial traditions, funeral rituals, when Mother suddenly said, "Get up! You can't sit in that chair. That's your father's favorite chair. He may be using it right now."

Bewildered, I moved to another chair and asked what she meant. This did not augur well for her decision to continue living in the house alone. My mother believes wholeheartedly in a hodge-podge world of Taoism, Confucianism, Buddhism, and animism, a universe filled with bureaucratic gods, ghosts, demons, and potentially malevolent wildcard spirits. I could imagine the scenario after I left: she'd be barricading herself behind her bedroom door each night, afraid to come out till morning light dispelled her fears if she thought Father's ghost was roaming the house in the dark hours.

149

To my dubious relief, Mother explained that Chinese folklore claimed the dead returned at night on a temporary basis during the first seven-sevens (49 days) after their death. The sun had set and I was about to invade my father's spiritual space. She told me I could sit in Father's favorite chairs (he had two: one in the kitchen/dining area and one in the sitting room) as much as I liked when the sun was up.

"Oh Mother," I said, indulgently, "You and your superstitions!"

"It's true!" Mother said. "When a person dies, the soul hovers about the body or the house, in the form of a moth or other insect, or even a smell. Your third cousin, when she died, came back as a cicada. Her children either did not believe or were ignorant. One of them smacked it with a flyswatter and broke its left hind leg. Later, when they consulted a medium to ask if their mother was happy and had all she needed in the Other World, the medium said Third Cousin was lame now because when she came home to visit, someone broke her left leg."

On the day of the funeral, Mother noticed a cricket in the bathroom. "Don't hurt that cricket," she warned us. "Let it stay as long as it likes. That's your father's soul taking a last look around before he sets out for the Yellow River."

"I didn't know Father was that fond of the bathroom!" Elder Brother LeeLang joked.

A year ago, our father's kidneys had failed. The renal dialysis that cleaned his blood and kept him alive had overstressed his heart. He suffered a stroke and lapsed into a coma in the hospital from which he never woke. He died two days later, on a Wednesday morning. Elder Brother LeeLang set the funeral for Saturday so that the overseas children could reach home in time. I reached home on Friday afternoon, after a numbing succession of planes and airports.

"Has LeeLang washed Father's face?" I asked my sister-in-law when she picked me up at Subang Airport. I knew this was a most important ritual and I hoped I did not have to witness it. I did not wish to look on my dead father. I wanted to remember him alive. Mother used to go over burial rituals so that we would know how to bury her and/or father properly if she wasn't alive to direct and take care of things herself. She emphasized the importance of the "face-washing ritual"; one cannot start out on the journey to the Chinese underworld with a dirty face. Only a son or grandson (natural or adopted is acceptable, but never a daughter or female descendant) can perform this crucial task. Hence the importance of male children in Chinese culture.

The other thing to remember, Mother stressed, was that a male could perform the "face-washing ritual" only two times in his life or he risked losing all his life's luck. In Chinese belief, there is nothing as spiritually contaminating and unclean as a fresh corpse. Also considered unclean and polluting, though not on the same scale, are menstrual blood and a woman after she gives birth. The Chinese consider anything that disrupts the order of the family or the body as "unclean," whether it is entry or exit. Birth does both—the newborn exits its mother's body and enters the family. It has to be purified by being bathed in water infused with *lingchee* grass or pomelo leaves. A woman on her wedding day must also be purified by bathing in water with pomelo leaves, for she exits her birth family and enters her husband's.

When I arrived at my parents' house, the entire front had been transformed. A temporary zinc canopy had been hastily erected to stretch out from the carport and over part of the street. Two huge oval "death lanterns," white rice paper stretched over bamboo, flanked the gate on eight-foot-high poles. They bore the characters for the deceased's family name, "Tham," and his age plus a bonus of 3 years in blue ink. (Father was 76; his death lanterns said 79.) The entryway to the makeshift "lying-in-state" parlor was lined with fresh flowers and floral wreaths, expressions of sympathy from friends, but mainly from business colleagues of my siblings. "Twenty-four bouquets!" Mother said, after the funeral. "Your father loved flowers. He would have been so proud; his sons are respected in the business world."

My aunt Lin Kam greeted me and led me to the temporary altar in the front. It was covered by a tablecloth of yellow silk with embroidered cabalistic Taoist symbols, its soiled appearance testifying to heavy usage. Or the *lama* priest did not mind dirt. Or both. She told me to light three joss sticks at one of the pair of tall red candles burning on the altar. I bowed to the 8-by-10-inch black-and-white photograph of my father, taken when he was forty, and stood them upright in the incense urn before the photograph. Joss sticks and stick stubs crowded the urn. Many had come and paid their respects before me. Elder Brother LeeLang told me that Father had pointed out this photograph, which had hung on our wall these many years, to him and said to use it for his *"sam jiew, yi yat,"* third morning of two days, meaning death.

Flanking the altar were four-foot-tall paper mannequins, a man-servant and a maidservant, dressed in Ching dynasty clothes, each holding a tray. The maid bore a Chinese teapot and teacups; the man held a pack of Rothman's cigarettes and a box of matches on his. My father had given up smoking twenty years before—I suppose the thought was that he could now smoke to his heart's desire since smoking could no longer affect his health. For my grandfather, a replica of an opium pipe was presented.

I bowed to my father's photograph and placed three incense sticks in the urn to pay my respects to his memory. Though I had converted to Judaism many years ago, upon my marriage, it did not bother me to perform the rituals. My religion forbade worship of graven images and idols. I did not believe my father was present in the picture on the altar. I did not believe he was in the wax-like gray body in the coffin behind the altar. I knew I did it to honor both my parents (so my mother would not feel she had failed to raise filial children), to honor my father, his memory that was achingly alive in his family now, knowing that it would diminish as entropy shreds us and dying stars wink out one by one. I would perform the rituals to honor the position of "father" that he had filled, to acknowledge our relationship. We were two bodies forever bound by an accident of birth.

Mother was not pleased that I had come home for the funeral. She had wanted me to stay away and not get polluted by the corpse. Youngest sister ChoyChoy, who lived near me in Virginia, was pregnant and due any day. Mother fretted that by tradition, I should now stay away from Choy for 100 days in order not to mix pollutions and risk bad luck.

Mother had turned to Brother LeeLang, as the child *in situ*, for making decisions about the funeral arrangements. He was the only one of her children still living in the vicinity, in the same country. The burden of caring for our aging parents had fallen on him—true, we all cared, we all telephoned, we sent money home. But we were not there to drive Father to the doctor or the hospital, to fill his prescriptions, to take Mother for eyeglasses and to her doctors. LeeLang had had to be main crutch, emergency squad, peace maker, chief errand boy, constantly called on by one parent or the other with a new need or an old complaint. Luckily for us, he had been raised with his duties as "First Son" impressed well and early on him. He accepted it as his responsibility and never complained. For which we felt equal parts guilt and gratitude.

Mother had two objectives when they rushed out to buy a grave plot. It should have good *feng shui* (wind water) to bring good *joss*, good fortune to the descendants; and it should not cost too much. She was pleased over the grave site they purchased, a double lot so she could be buried there later. She told me proudly that she had talked the price of the plot down three hundred dollars. LeeLang had seen to the ordering and delivery of all the things Mother said were necessary for sending Father's soul to the Chinese afterlife. He had arranged for the services of a Taoist priest (and two assistant chanters, plus two musicians) to chant the prayers and perform the proper rituals for the passage of the dead for three nights. He had taken Mother to select the coffin. He had ordered all the artifacts and paraphernalia necessary for Father to maintain a proper living standard in the afterlife: a huge seven-foot-wide by six-foot-tall paper mansion with garden and balustraded walks, two paper servants to wait on him in the mansion, a red Mercedes automobile with chauffeur (Would a Ching dynasty-clad chauffeur know how to drive? I wondered privately), and a Hellivision and VCR, with VHS tapes on which Mother had written the titles of Father's favorite movies. The funeral supply shop had Hell Passports and even airplane tickets. LeeLang did not buy those. He said he figured we didn't want Father's ghost wandering and lost in America looking for us. And twelve chests of gold and silver ingots with stacks of currency issued by the Bank of Hell. Father could be as extravagant as he wished now.

Mourning garments could not be purchased. Tradition decreed that they must be rough-cut, unhemmed, and stitched in haste when the need was real, when death had occurred. Our mourning garments were a rush job by Mother, her sister, and a cousin. Members of the immediate family are chief mourners, and all must wear full black for a hundred days. During the funeral rituals, male mourners wear a white mourning tunic made of coarse cotton over their blacks. They wear a two-cornered hat made from the same white cotton as the tunic. Female relatives wear white cotton hoods that drape down their backs. Traditionally, mourners also had to don burlap garments over their whites and blacks. But the burlap had gone out of use and we were given little squares of burlap to safety pin to our sleeves as a nod to the past.

The Taoist service began at sunset with loud clashing of cymbals, beating of a small drum, and ringing of a nastily nasal string instrument for which I have no name. It lasted up to midnight. We had to put on our mourner's garments for ceremonial rituals at various times during the service. When the priest came to parts of his prayers where he listed the descendants of the deceased, he needed us physically present to show to the spirits he was propitiating. I remembered being kept awake all night as a child by the noise of the keening mourners and the discordant music when our next-door neighbor died. "Aren't the services supposed to last till dawn?" I asked LeeLang.

"Yes, they used to," was his reply. "But the government passed a law and now all the hullabaloo has to end by midnight. I guess they got too many complaints. I'm just as glad I don't have to kneel and rise and kneel and rise all night long. My poor back can't take too much of that." My usually serious brother was grinning now. "Another good thing—they got rid of that dreadful screeching-to-wake-the-dead bit. I remember I had to do it at Grandmother's funeral. Made me feel like a bloody fool, throwing myself on the ground and yelling, 'Come back, Grandma! Please don't leave us!' I sure would have run like hell out of there if she had popped up out of the coffin, saying, 'Huh? You called?' When I go, I want a simple quiet funeral. A Christian-style funeral. None of this superstitious stuff. It's downright undignified!"

Mother did not wear mourning and she did not participate in the service. She greeted friends and relatives and organized the food and drinks and other supplies needed by the living and the dead. My mother always has a Chinese logic to her actions. Out of curiosity, I asked her why she was not wearing mourning garments. I remembered a neighbor, Mrs. Ho, in full mourning whites and burlap, throwing herself in the dirt at her husband's funeral. "Age has its privilege," Mother said. "I have passed 60 years. Your father and I have both passed 60; we have eaten the *sau thoy*, peach of longevity, together. We have children and grandchildren. No need to wear mourning when the life has been long and the duty has been done. When a person has lived as long and full a life as your father has, there is little cause for me to mourn."

The Friday night service ended with teleporting the funeral

supply shop's best buys to the fourth dimension by the burning method: the paper mansion, chests of gold and money, the paper servants, even his favorite pair of slippers, and naturally, the *pièce de résistance*, the Mercedes motor car, complete with license plate and chauffeur. Aunt Lin Kam and Cousin Mui both bought lottery tickets or Lotto with the license numbers, and we were glad to hear, later, that they did win several hundred dollars each.

Saturday morning came, with clouds dark and threatening, grumbling of thunder behind the eastern foothills. Mother grew increasingly worried as the thunder came closer and louder. Finally, she hurried into the backyard and talked to her gods. "God of Sky, God of Wind and Rain, I'm petitioning you. Hold back the rain until after the funeral. Whatever my husband has said or done to offend, I cry pardon and beg your forgiveness for him. I seldom ask favors, I'm a good gods-in-my-heart person, devoted always. Please grant me this favor. Do not rain on his funeral. Let him sleep peaceful and dry."

My mother has a very personal relationship with her gods. She believes they listen to her and will actively intercede for her. She keeps pointing out to us that her faith is often justified. As in the present case. The rain did not come down until Father was buried and we were back in the house.

"Now remember, LeeLang has 'washed the face' twice. He cannot do it a third time," Mother said to us all. "When my *sam jiew, yi yat*, third morning of two days, comes, CheeLung will have to do it for me. And it has to be 'bought' water. Water you buy from a public faucet or the street."

"I thought Uncle Yuen bought water from the little temple when Grandfather died," I said.

"No, no!" Mother was shocked. "You cannot go near a temple with a death in the family. Chief mourners are polluted by the corpse. You offend the gods with your pollution. No, you buy water by taking a pail of water to the road, you set it down and then buy it from the spirit of the place with a few cents. You leave the coins by the roadside."

"Do we still put a silver coin in the mouth?" I asked, remembering another tradition.

"Well, most people do. I completely forgot for your father."

Mother was disconcerted for a moment. "Anyway, it's just as well. Your grandmother refused to keep her coin in her mouth. Three times I stuck it on her tongue, and three times she spit it out. She was always difficult. Even dead, she had to be difficult."

Father's funeral was set for ten o'clock. A little before, the musicians arrived with the Taoist priest and his assistants. They busied themselves with lighting joss sticks and candles, and burning *po* papers to pacify and appease any spirits Father's soul might encounter on the shadow road to the Underworld. We put on our mourning garments and were given incense sticks to hold. "Everyone turn your backs. We're taking down the altar," the priest's aide called out. When we could turn around again, all the clutter around the coffin was gone. The priest led us in a procession counterclockwise around the coffin. We circled the coffin three times and were told to have our last look at Father and then to line up by the hearse.

There is a morbid curiosity in us that is almost impossible to resist when bidden to look upon the dead. We know that someday, we too will reach this end. I looked through the coffin's glass lid at my father's face. Unlike American undertakers, Malaysian undertakers do no cosmetic work on the dead. My father's body had been filled with formaldehyde and his face above his graveclothes was a wax-gray effigy's. I acknowledged silently that he was gone and I was one generation closer now to death. I looked on death's guise and found I was not afraid. My father's dying had been natural and orderly. I hoped mine would be, too.

"Turn your backs. Do not look. We are closing up the coffin," the assistant said as he hurried back to help with the process. We obediently looked the other way though I noticed LeeLang was sneaking a peep. When my grandfather died, I had been too young to be permitted full participation or observation of the funeral. When Grandmother died, I was in America. My father's was the first funeral I witnessed completely and with full awareness. I asked the priest later why we were not permitted to look at these various points of the rituals.

"If your luck is high, you can look and no harm from it," the priest explained. "But if your luck is low, looking can attract the attention of a wild one from the spirit world. When a person dies and his spirit is about to cross over, the spirit world comes very close to the physical world. Wild denizens of the spirit world sense these entry/exit openings and are attracted to them. They come in hordes and will latch on to any living person whose luck is low and bring evil influences to them."

After the coffin was loaded into the hearse and all the tribute flowers piled on top, we had to wait for the raising of the "hero's banner." The homonym for "hero" in Chinese is "daughter" and "red" so if a dead man was the father of a daughter and had a son-in-law, he was entitled to have a "hero's banner" flying before his funeral procession, his triumphal march to the grave. There is a great emphasis on natural order and decorum in Chinese rituals. Since I was First Daughter, my husband (had he been present) would have been the one to raise the long pole bearing a long, red cloth with the names of all the sons-in-law. Since Joe was in China on business, the next in birth order was my sister Su'en ChoyNgor. Her husband David was directed by the priest to raise the hero's banner and walk before the hearse down our street. I thought of my husband's bad back and was relieved that he was not available to perform this ritual.

The priest placed us as chief mourners behind the hearse and signaled for the procession to begin. As we walked behind the slow-moving hearse, the band—cymbals, drum, trumpet, saxophone (quiet till then)—burst into a brassy funeral march. Or I thought it was a funeral march until it registered on my startled mind that the tune was "Amazing Grace." We had been expecting the traditional, heart-dragging, whining dirge of Chinese funeral music. "Oh dear, how modern!" SiewLan, LeeLang's wife, was trying to muffle a giggle. "Good Lord! They sound like a New Orleans brass band," David, my English brother-in-law and a jazz aficionado, said, highly diverted. As the four musicians swung from "Amazing Grace" into "Nearer My God to Thee," the cultural incongruity brought laughter bubbling up in me, and, as I could see from their faces, in my siblings and their spouses, along with the knowledge that it was a dreadfully inappropriate time for laughter.

LeeLang's face was a pond with wind riffling across from different directions. "I thought they were supposed to be a traditional band, playing traditional Chinese funeral music. That's not traditional and it's definitely not Chinese!" But being LeeLang, he was philosophical about it. "At least they're only a little bit off-pitch.

And their music won't give us nightmares, like real Chinese funeral music." At this point, we fell apart and became hysterical.

It was a good thing that Mother had walked only a few steps alongside the hearse, as a symbolic "sending off," and was now back in the house worrying about washing the floor and ritually cleaning the house of pollution. Onlookers must have thought we were grief-stricken and most filial indeed as we walked tremblingly behind the hearse, faces bent to the ground, hands fisted in our mouths.

Yet it felt right to be sending our father off with tears and laughter. He had often displayed a sense of humor, an appreciation for the ridiculous, except when his mistresses and his preferred lifestyle made demands he could not meet. He would have laughed at the incongruity too, had it been someone else's funeral.

At the end of our street, the hearse stopped. We knelt to face the house we had left and the priest chanted a final farewell on behalf of the dead. Since the cemetery was 25 miles away and it would take hours to walk, another old ritual had been modernized. LeeLang had provided transport in the welcome shape of a bus waiting discreetly at the end of the street. We boarded it and rode to the cemetery in air-conditioned comfort, dabbing sweat from our necks and faces. It was the usual 90 degrees Fahrenheit, 99 percent humidity Malaysian day.

At the cemetery, we had to pay respects to the guardian spirit of the land. The guardian had to be informed that our father was a new resident and entreated to extend the usual courtesies and protection. Chinese cemeteries are always located on hills unless no hills are available. In order for *ley* and *chi*, power emanations from nature and people, to flow and be renewed, the land of graves must be on slopes. Low, flat grave sites, where water pools and stagnates, are considered the worst wind-water sites of all.

We left the bus and walked up the hill. The road wound through the oldest part of the cemetery. Here, the graves were large mounds with balustraded walls and tall marble headstones with photos of the dead lithographed on them. The pastel walls on the slopes looked like the houses of a little Italian town. Except these dwellings were not as kempt, their grass tall and wild. Chinese cemeteries only look presentable once a year, at ChingMing, when the Chinese visit the graves of their ancestors with grass-shears and offerings of food and Bank of Hell money. It bothered me to see signs of vandalism on the tombs. Many had their lithographed portraits removed or defaced, some partially smashed. I wondered what malice, what anger had to be expressed against the impersonal, no longer provoking, dead?

We were soaked with sweat by the time we reached the new section of the cemetery, where we found the hearse waiting. Also the priest and his crew, as well as the grinning musicians. They had taken a shortcut in their jeep. As if to vindicate their reputation, the band called forth the death wails of tortured small animals from their instruments; in other words, they played a traditional Chinese dirge. Standing around the edge of the freshly dug hole that would soon house our father's body, all lightness left us. A darkness settled over our minds, a heaviness that crushed our spirits and numbed us from feeling.

The priest bade us turn our backs while the coffin was slid on two round poles into the pit. Then we were asked to approve the *feng shui* (wind-water) aspects of the coffin's position. "What you want," the priest said, "is the coffin to be aligned so that your father will have a pleasant prospect before him, with nothing, like another's tombstone, to obstruct his view." So we tried to place ourselves in Father's particular position at that point and had the gravediggers adjust the coffin so that its line of sight stretched out to hills, valley, green grass, and distant trees.

Next came the rooster ceremony. As First Son, LeeLang had to stand on the edge of the pit, at the foot of the grave. The priest produced a rooster and circled the grave, chanting blessings over it. The rooster was passive and silent all this while, its golden eye petrified with fright. Finally, the priest checked with LeeLang that he was ready to receive the rooster, and he flung the bird across the grave-pit to Brother. LeeLang caught the rooster with both hands. To drop the rooster would have brought much ill-luck.

"Good thing I used to play rugby!" LeeLang said.

The priest removed the trembling rooster from his arms and replaced it in the covered basket. Then he called across the open grave for us to strip off our mourning garments, and to toss a clod of earth into the grave. "Now walk away, do not look back. Halfway down the hill, remove your socks and leave them by the road." He had explained earlier that casting off our socks was a symbolic shedding, separating ourselves from, the dead.

I understood the symbolism of the act but I knew that, though we could separate ourselves from our father physically, there was no way we, his children, could ever disengage our psyches from him. I was grateful for the three weeks I had spent with him, a month before his death; grateful I had gotten him to talk about himself to me. Talking to his children was a rare thing for my father. During those three weeks, I learned things about his life that even Mother had never known. I learned how my grandparents' neglect and the harsh economic circumstances of his childhood and youth had shaped him into the faithless husband, the irresponsible parent we had had to pretend we respected all his life. I was glad I had been able to tell him while he was alive that I loved him and that his only failing in my eyes was his unkindness to Mother. This he denied vehemently. "I have always been good to your mother," he said. "All our disagreements come from her being such an unreasonable woman."

I regretted that we had not spent more time together, accepted the fact that our relationship was irrevocably frozen by his death, the emotional distance between us irreducible now. As we walked away, I could hear the thuds of shovelfuls of earth landing on wood. There is something very final about the sound.

26

Final Days

After Father's funeral, when everyone except the immediate family had said their final condolences and gone, quiet fell on the house, welcome as tree-shade after hours of glaring sun, soothing as aloe on sunburned skin. We were sitting in the living room, silent with our separate thoughts, our responses to the man we had just buried. I was remembering the time he had disowned me, when I was eighteen, when he had told me I was no daughter of his. I thought of another unreasonable father who had disowned his daughter, King Lear. Pondered the nature of love. Had I loved my father "like salt"? Mother had loved him like salt, and vinegar, and cayenne peppers, and wormwood, I thought.

Her brisk voice brought us out of our reveries. "I bought him the best *sau yee*, burial clothes," Mother said. "It was coffee-colored, a brocade gown with a silvery vest. It cost over six hundred dollars. Your father would have liked it. He loved to dress well."

The clothes of a vanished Chinese dynasty, a Manchu lord's gown and hat, had completed death's work in changing the body in the coffin to a stranger's. I had looked at the body in the coffin and found, in its face, a clay replica of my father's.

I thought of my cousin-sister, KeatWah. She had told me on our walk down cemetery hill of her father's reactions after viewing Father's body; how he had asked that his family not bury him in the traditional burial garments. Cousin-Uncle YeeFong had been very brave, for him. He had paid final respects, performed the traditional "viewing of the body." Since childhood, he had a phobia of Manchu-clad bodies. They reminded him of Chinese horror movies, where corpses stalked from their coffins and terrorized the countryside, killing people.

"The cloth shoes were too big for his feet." Mother spoke again. "I asked for a smaller pair but the coffin-shop man said all the shoes came 'one size fits all.' He said I could choose the color and the quality; they come in different quality silks or plain cotton. The poor buy cotton gowns. I got your father the best silk. I wanted him to hold his head high in the World Below."

She told us about the last days before Father's stroke and death. "He knew his time had come. Last week, after he slept for three days, he was very alert on Saturday. He said to me: 'Wui kong farn jhew, it's my departing light's reflection.' He said it twice that day. And on Monday, at one o'clock in the morning, he was rummaging in his closet. I was wakened by the click of mothballs rolling on wood. I said, 'What are you doing?'

"He said, 'I'm getting dressed.'

"I said, 'Whatever for?'

"He said, 'I'm getting ready to go.'

"'Don't be silly,' I said, 'It's too early. We don't have to go to the dialysis clinic until six A.M. Go back to sleep.' He listened to me. He took off his t-shirt and let me take him back to his bed. I didn't realize at the time he meant he was getting ready to depart. I had the coffin-shop man put that shirt he chose on him, under his burial clothes, since he wanted to wear it for his final journey."

A little later, Mother said, "The dying see things from the other world. Two months before, he told me a little child was following him around, in the house and when we went out. He asked if I saw the kid. I told him he was imagining things. 'Tell the child you have no enmity or guilt between you and it will go away.' He never mentioned the child again. I think it must have left after I said that.

"Another time, he told me there was a huge rooster and a duck looking at him from the back yard. I looked at where he pointed and saw nothing, only sunlight on the cement. I said, 'Nonsense! It's only the shadows from the banana tree.'

"Many nights, he called out and woke me from my sleep in the middle of the night. 'Open the door,' he said. 'There's someone knocking at the door. He's got a package for me.' I would tell him firmly, 'Nobody delivers packages at three A.M. You've been dreaming. Go back to sleep.' I hid the door keys. I was afraid he might open the door while I was sleeping and let thieves and robbers into the house.

"Another time, he pointed to the solid wall and said, 'There's a hole in the wall. I can see mice coming in through the hole.' You know me, I've very little gall, I've always been afraid of the dark. Two years earlier, I would have been terrified by his words. Luckily, I am much bolder now—since I accepted Buddhism. When I was visiting America, the Buddhist priest there explained to me that the spirits of the Other World are not evil, and that they will not harm you if you are pure of heart and speak to them respectfully, and without fear. I knew your father had one foot in the Shadow World and was seeing things from the Shadows.

"He was afraid of dying. Like his mother, who took to her bed and called for the doctor every time she heard one of her peers had passed away. Once, he asked how much longer did I think he had. I told him, 'When a person's time to die comes, it comes, and nothing can change it. There is nothing to fear. Even the Queen of England's father had to die when his time came. And he had hundreds of doctors trying to prolong his life.' I think this comforted him.

"I was not happy when LeeLang offered to fetch the Christian priest to the hospital to baptize him if he wished. What would I do, where would I go, if he had changed religions and ended up in a Christian cemetery? Your father showed some consideration for my feelings at the end, when he told LeeLang, 'No baptism. Your mother wouldn't like it.' He knew we couldn't be buried together if he died a Christian. My heart is eased now we have bought the double plot. It is fitting we should be together at the end; after all, we've been husband and wife these fifty-one years. Not that they were such good years."

On my visit the month before, I had asked my father the same question as my brother. We knew Father had been going to the local Baptist church before his kidneys failed. We both wanted to offer him the solace of Christianity if he wanted it. Father had always claimed religions were all the same and that he did not believe in any one of them. I asked him if he wanted me to talk Mother into accepting his conversion. "No," he said, shaking his head with a slight smile. "I am not really a believer. I went to the church because

I like roast pork and they serve very good roast pork after their services."

I think he lied then. I think he did derive comfort from the
more forgiving rationality of Judeo-Christian theology. I believe he
did not want to deprive Mother of the rituals and practice of her
faith, knew she needed them to ease her heart when he left her. He
knew she would have taken his burial in a Christian cemetery
(where she could not follow) as the ultimate rejection. In his careless
way, he had loved her though he had given her a cat-and-dog life
and had been constantly unfaithful to her.

Days later, sorting through his things, his many locked drawers, Mother and I found a lease on a furnished house. He had rented
the house from age sixty-three to sixty-five. I had to laugh. Long
after we believed he had given up his womanizing ways, my irre-
pressible father had kept a woman on the side for two full years.

Coming Up Short

My uncle Yuen tried to cheat his customers when he inherited
Grandfather's furniture store—had his workers save wood on
the length of beds they made. Shorted customers complained,
even after he delivered regulation-sized replacements.
Before he declared bankruptcy, he sold one of his specials
to Mother, at "discount for a relative."
I learned this thirty years later,
after my father died.

In the quiet nights after Father's funeral, I noticed
the shortness of that special bed, my pillow squashed
against the headboard, my toes touching the footboard.
Mother told me about her brother's scam.

I recalled my uncle's face: an honest-seeming face
with square-cut brow, clean-shaven jaw,
diffident smile, thoughtful eyes. His was not
the face of a man who sold six-inch shorted
beds, not the face of a man who embezzled and
lost a subsequent job as a manager.
He seldom spoke, busy always with his own thoughts.

These days, my uncle travels to small towns, sells
men's socks at foldaway one-night stands.
He should have sold coffins. Sleepers
in the earth do not raise their arms or
open their mouths to ask,
"Why is this bed different from all others?"

A man with skimpy integrity must live
with suspicions skittering in his skull, expecting
all to be like himself, ready to cheat him if they could, as
he would himself if only he could figure out a way
to do it without getting caught again.

"How could you sleep in this uncomfortable bed
for thirty years?" I asked, as my elbow hit the head
board again. "Beside your father's infidelities,
your uncle's gambling addiction, and his stupid
dishonesty, a short bed was a small thing
to endure," Mother said. "I got used to it."

27

The Lore of the Dead

"On the seventh day, the dead soul goes to the Yellow River," Mother said, "in the World Below, to wash his hands. It is then that he realizes he is dead, for his skin will smell of death and he can see river bank and reeds through his hands."

The first three weeks after death is the period of the "lost and wandering soul." Chinese lore has it that the dead soul is still attached to earthly things, people, and places; its presence can be detected by unusual phenomena like a weird smell, an insect indoors.

"When the coffin was brought to the house, a smell of cockroaches filled the house," Mother told me after the funeral. "And again on the second day. I smelled it but I thought it was my imagination. Then your aunt smelled it too. She said, 'Elder Sister, you really should fumigate your house. It has so many roaches they are smelling really bad.' At first, I thought the hospital had forgotten to embalm your father. I went and checked but there was no smell around the coffin. The roach smell was only in the kitchen and living room, his two favorite rooms."

My mother is convinced that the rank smell of cockroaches that invaded the house twice was Father; that the cricket in the bathroom, too, was Father. I asked how she would manage, living in the house alone, with her beliefs. I had to return to America.

"Don't worry. I'm not afraid to stay in the house alone. It's only

167

on the 'Night of the Returning Soul,' the twenty-first night, that I am a little scared. I will ask a friend to stay with me. That night, I will prepare food and wine for your father and the Yamen Guards, Horse-Face and Cow-Head, who will escort him up from the Underworld for his farewell visit. My friend and I will lock ourselves in my bedroom upstairs. Your father will visit his bedroom and other parts of the house. I wouldn't want to meet them. Not that your father would harm me but the Yamen Guards and any friends he brings from the spirit world could take offense and ill-wish me. Best to take no chances."

"You mean you'll have to hide in your room all night?" I asked, not reassured by her plan. "Why don't we ask Elder Brother to keep you company that night?"

"No, no, not LeeLang," Mother was quite agitated now. "He doesn't believe in these things, he will disregard me and walk around the house at the wrong time and bump into the spirit demons and ruin his life! Anyway, it is not all night. Before midnight, I will throw a pair of scissors on the floor to warn them it's time to leave. Spirits do not like forged iron. That will be the last time his soul wanders around. After that, it will be taken into the place of ancestors and bound up in the ancestral tablet on the altar. Then I'll have only thieves and robbers to worry about."

The day after the funeral, Mother remembered she had omitted to warn us not to use sharp instruments. "*Aiyah!* I hope none of you were cutting anything. Chief mourners must not use a knife or scissors or even a needle when the corpse is present in the house. Sharp things can cause the dead body to bleed—his soul will suffer the torment of the Blood River before it can proceed onward. It's the punishment for 'bringing red' (blood pollution) into the World Below."

"Oh Mother," I said, "another superstition to tie us up in knots!"

"No, no," Mother said earnestly, "This is true. I myself saw it with my own eyes when I was young. My God-Brother died in his sleep. When your father and I went to pay our respects, his body was clean and dry. In the back of the house, we found his wife chopping up roast pork. I said, 'God-Brother's Wife, you must not use a chopper until the body is buried!' She poohed-poohed me, didn't believe in superstitions, she said. When we looked in the coffin for final farewell, blood had leaked out over the front of God-Brother's burial tunic. There was blood from his nose and mouth. Because of his wife, his ghost must have been tormented for months in the Blood River!"

I had never heard of the Blood River before. Mother explained that it was a special place in the World Below, a special part of Chinese Hell formed by blood from menstruating women. The dead soul sinks in it, it burns him; he swallows blood clots, screams for help. But no friendly spirit can help him. All good spirits shun the Blood River, for menstrual blood is extremely polluting; it is as unclean as fresh corpses, for it is dead fetuses—it should have made babies.

"You know, I completely forgot!" Mother said, conscience-stricken. "I sliced an orange the afternoon after your father died. I hope I haven't caused him to sit in the Blood River for a day." Being extremely practical, she did not let it bother her long. "Done is done. Too late to worry about it. Did I ever tell you the story of my god-father and the Unlucky Barber?"

Mother's story of the Unlucky Barber:
A comic tale of two corpses & three coffins

My godfather was a medicine man. He made balms and unguents that were famed for their effectiveness on rheumatic aches and pains. Such a pity his sons and daughters-in-law burned his medicine formula book after he died. They felt that since he always carried it in his pocket, he would want it with him in the World Below. Oh, there was such an upset when he died. You see, he died in a barber's chair where he had gone for a haircut.

Funny thing was—the local fortune-teller had been shaved by the barber that morning and he noticed an astral cloud over the barber's head. He said to the barber, "You are going to have trouble with the police today. Better close up shop now, go home and stay there if you want to evade this cloud hanging over your head." The barber laughed. "I don't steal and I don't cheat. Why should I have trouble with the police?"

That afternoon, my godfather came to the barber to have his head shaved. He was a *botak*, a bald-head by choice. While he was in the barber's chair, he died; we think of a heart attack. When the police came, they arrested the barber and threw him in jail while they investigated the cause of Godfather's sudden death. Because he had no identification on him, Godfather's body was sent to the hospital morgue.

By coincidence, another old man, also a bald-head, had died earlier in the hospital. When his sons came to claim the body, they were given my godfather's, instead. They were very careless; they should have made sure it was their father's body. Meanwhile, my godfather's family grew worried when the old man did not come home at nightfall. No one had telephones then. They ran all over town to relatives and friends, asking if anyone knew his whereabouts. It was not till noon of the next day that they heard about the barber who had been arrested because a man had died during a shave in his shop. They rushed to the hospital morgue, asked anxiously if a bald-headed old man had been brought there. Shown the one bald corpse, they said, "No, no, that's not our father. Are you sure this is the only dead, bald old man you have?"

Pressed, the morgue attendant remembered that he had released another bald old male corpse to a Chen family the previous day, remembered hearing the funeral was that afternoon. My godfather's sons ran all the way from the hospital to the cemetery and they were just in time. The Chen funeral procession was starting up the cemetery hill.

"Stop! Stop!" they yelled. "You've got the wrong corpse." The funeral stopped at these horrifying words. After much screaming and shouting, the Chen family agreed to open the coffin. They were most unhappy to find my godfather's corpse in their father's coffin. Back to town they ran, to buy a new coffin and to claim their own father. Here is where my godfather's sons made a terrible mistake. They should have bought the first coffin from the Chens and buried their father without disturbing him further. Instead, they took his body back to the house and installed him in a new coffin. It is very bad joss to re-open a coffin, worse *joss* to move a corpse unnecessarily. From that day, their family fortunes declined.

The first coffin was abandoned on the hillside by both families and it stayed there for years. Nobody wanted a used coffin, extremely bad joss. For months the town talked about the unlucky barber, jailed for three days for no fault of his, how he should have listened to the fortune-teller's warning.

"Seems to me the barber wasn't that unlucky," I observed. "He was still alive. The unlucky one was your godfather; he died."

"Yes, but he was an old man," Mother said serenely. "Dying is not a bad thing and he had a good death, a fast death, without prolonged suffering or illness. It is the living one should worry about, not the dead."

28

Bare Feet & Broken Glass

Tanam lallang, tak akan tumbuh padi.

When you plant grass, you won't get rice.

—Malay proverb

I did not know there was an uncultivated grass field in my mind, a place I avoided, a place covered with sharp-edged *lallang* that repelled thought, a subject marked "taboo," not to talk about, not to think about; until my publisher pointed it out. He noticed that I write about Indian immigrants, about the Chinese I grew up with, but that I barely mention the Malays who make up the majority of Malaysia's population. We were taught Malay as a second language in our English education schools. Indonesians speak the same language but call it Indonesian. In the early 1970s, Malay replaced English as the medium of education. Strange to realize that I met and talked with Malays in Malay almost daily, yet this part of my life was sealed off from my thinking and my writing. It was a habit trained into me from early days. I had become unaware of its existence, so deeply had I been conditioned.

* * *

Do not talk about the Malays.

* * *

It has been three weeks that I have been trying to write this chapter, about the major strand of Malaysian society with whom I was in almost daily contact in school and at the university. I have found myself cleaning house, rearranging furniture, anything, rather than sit down to think and write about the *bumiputeras* or "princes of the earth" as the Malays have called themselves from the 1960s on. In recent guidebooks to Malaysia, the term *bumiputera* is translated less accurately but more democratically as "sons of the soil."

I had little contact with Malays as a child. At the beginning of school holidays, Grandfather Au came and took us, brother LeeLang and I, to stay with him for two weeks in his furniture shop. I looked forward with great anticipation to the only vacation we had all year. First, there was the trip itself. We would ride the public bus to Bunting, twenty-two miles from Kelang. Nose pressed to the glass, I'd watch the countryside passing before my eyes. The nicest part about being with Grandfather was that he never nagged. Mother would have said, "Don't touch that window; you don't know who may have pressed their nose and mouth there. It may be full of germs!" I loved the peaceful look of the countryside our bus passed through; coconut trees and clusters of brown wooden houses on stilts with an occasional water buffalo dragging a plow through a flooded field with a Malay man steering the plow behind it. On the ride home, I would see Malay women in conical straw hats with their *sarongs* hitched up to their knees, bending and bending to plant rice seedlings. It was as picturesque as the postcards and colorful Western-style calendars we never had money to buy. Mother always got a free calendar at New Year's from the grocer. It had a picture of the god of longevity or a Hong Kong movie star, with a stack of days. She would tear off a leaf a day. They were the only art on our walls: movie stars from past years' calendars.

I grew up in a lane with Chinese and Indian neighbors. I met Malays only when I went to school. My first Malay friend was called Hamidah, in Forms One and Two (grades seven and eight). I remember visiting her house by the railroad tracks after school, riding home with her on our bicycles. The friendship faded as we grew older, perhaps due naturally to diminished common interests or because we had absorbed the poison of our adults' attitudes.

I knew the Malays were mainly farmers and fishermen, sometimes chauffeurs for the rich. They lived in *kampongs*, villages; their houses were made of wood and raised on stilts, for better air-flow and safety from tigers prowling the jungle's edge. Their homes were always tastefully decorated, tranquil with fresh flowers, and uncluttered, unlike Chinese homes which were crowded with every possession the family ever owned. I remember being amazed at how spacious a small house could be when I visited my Malay friend, Hamidah. The other thing that surprised me in her home was that there was no toilet paper in the bathroom. She explained that Malays believed "toilet paper causes hemorrhoids!" and that washing with soap and water was better for the health.

Malaysian Countryside

On our bus ride to Bunting, we'd pass little mosques, brightly painted red and white or blue and white. They looked so serene with their onion-bulb domes and minarets. Later, I visited the newly built National Mosque when I was in college. It was ultra-modern: all geometric shapes and planes, with a roof of soaring triangles. I've often thought the architect must have been trying to fold an origami fan and on the fifth try, realized the creased paper was a concept for the roof of a modern building. Its incongruity in a town filled with domes is heightened by contrast with the 1917 Moorish-style railway station, which it faces across the street. We used to joke that our

Kuala Lumpur Railway Station, National Mosque Background

National Mosque looked like a railway station and that the Railway Station looked like a mosque. After this embrace of modernism, mosque architecture returned to the beloved Moorish style, with onion domes and minarets, like the new Sultan Salahuddin Mosque in Shah Alam, the largest in Asia and third largest in the world. I have visited the Mosque of Omar in Jerusalem and seen the Rock made holy by the Prophet's foot; I have seen the Chinese mosque in Xian, and the Uighers' Idkah mosque in Kashgar, among others. Each time, I have been captivated by the spacious quiet of the peaceful entrance court yard, always with a foot-washing pool, and the richly Persian carpeted prayer halls.

The solemn silence that pervades mosques, churches, and synagogues (religions with one god), is not found in Chinese temples, which are the focal points for bazaars. Prayer halls are crowded with statues of minor and major deities. The Kek Lok Si Temple in Penang which I visited not long ago had courtyards filled with the clamorous din of hawkers selling incense, candles, prayer-beads, souvenirs of Penang, clay buddhas, wind chimes, and ludicrously, plastic dog turds (made in Germany) for practical jokes. Also spinach for feeding the hundred-year-old tortoises in the third courtyard pond. Hindu temples, belonging to another multi-god religion, have an atmosphere similar to that of Chinese temples. At the Hindu shrine in Batu Cave, kiosks offer Indian curries, snacks, coconut drinks, even bags of peanuts to feed the sacred monkeys.

I knew Islam was the national religion. All Malays were Muslims. They did not like to mix with the other races, especially the Chinese who raised and ate pigs, an animal the Malays regarded as extremely unclean and polluting. Young Malays were warned by their *imam* (priest) and elders not to mingle with non-Muslims lest they become contaminated by worldly cultures. Today, Malay students going overseas for higher education are given lectures on how to avoid decadent Western influences and non-Malay ways of thought during their years of study in America, Europe, or Japan.

Malays are forbidden by law to convert to another religion. Should a Malay want to marry a non-Muslim, the would-be spouse must convert to Islam and be married by the *imam*. I discovered this when Joe (my husband) and I were planning our civil wedding. Joe had a friend, R.J., a fellow Peace Corps volunteer, who was in love with a Malay girl. To marry her, he had to convert to Islam and be circumcised. Muslim males are circumcised at age twelve whereas Jewish males are circumcised when they are eight days old, faithfully keeping the ritual begun by Abraham on his sons, Isaac and Ishmael. Ishmael, first ancestor of the Arabs, was believed to be twelve at the time.

This rite of passage is an elaborate celebration for Malays. The circumcision of a Malay prince is dramatized by a tableau in the National Museum of History: In the center of the court, with the Sultan and His Consort seated on their thrones, the prince stands with his *sarong* (cylindrical skirt) held extended. The court circumciser stands in the *sarong* with him and performs the surgery to remove the foreskin. Two court executioners stand behind the prince, with axes ready to remove the circumciser's head should his fingers slip and he remove anything more than foreskin. It is no longer customary to have court executioners, but guards of the royal household do stand by for a quick arrest in case of mistakes. Dealing with princes is risky business. "That was the most painful experience of my life," R.J. told us later. "It's going to be a while before I can perform my conjugal duties."

Joe and I were married by a Marriage Registrar under the

"Civil Marriage Ordinance of 1952." The Marriage Registrar was a Malay, Abdul Hamid bin (son of) Haji Abu Bakar. He had Joe raise his right hand and say "I do" to the question: "Do you, Joseph R. Goldberg, swear that you will not take another woman to wife unless you first divorce this woman, Hilary Tham, or you will be subject to five years in jail and/or one thousand dollars fine?" Then I raised my right hand and he asked, solemnly, "Do you, Hilary Tham, also known as Tham ChoyKam, swear you will not take another man for a husband unless you first divorce this man, Joseph R. Goldberg, or you will be subject to five years in jail and/or one thousand dollars fine?" And I said, equally seriously, "I do."

Mr. Hamid said we were the fifth couple to be married by him in 1971. Kuantan was a small town on the east coast of Malaya, its population mainly Malay fisherfolk. Since Muslims must be married by an *imam*, there was not much call for civil weddings. He gave us copies of our marriage certificate, a blue one for Joe, a pink one for me; and wished us a long and happy life together. He even tossed some rice on us as we left his office. Joe was laughing. He said, "Whatever happened to 'love, cherish, and obey'? I especially miss the 'obey your husband' part!"

"It is rather bottomline and unsentimental," I said. "I think I like the idea of your Jewish *ketubah* better." Joe had told me about the Jewish wedding contract, in which the man promises to cherish the woman and keep her in the style to which she is accustomed. "The style you're accustomed to would only cost me pennies," Joe had said jokingly. He also told me that the man had to promise to give the bride a herd of fifty goats should he divorce her. The woman only had to say "I do" to the question, "Do you accept this man's promises?" When we were married by a rabbi many years later in America, I found that the Jewish wedding contract was exactly as he had described it, with one slight modification: Joe could pay me the fair market price of fifty goats instead of fifty bleating live animals.

I read in the news, a few years ago, that an Australian couple, a visiting parson and his wife, had been arrested and jailed for subversion. They had discussed comparative religions with a Malay couple over dinner. It is a crime to discuss religion with a Malay. It is considered an attempt to seduce him/her away from Islam. After much negotiation and strong protest from the Australian government, the couple were freed and expelled from Malaysia.

* * *

Do not go among the Melayu people. They
are witch-doctors, bomohs. *They will make you do things*
you wouldn't do in your right mind.

The Melayu like the fair skin of Chinese
girl-children. They will kidnap you.

* * *

My mother had a friend, Mrs. Mah, whose daughter fell in love with a Malay man and married him, over the protests of her parents. "There is no talking sense into SauWan," Mrs. Mah fretted to my mother. "She is bewitched. She is like a sleepwalker these days. He must have given her a love potion." Later, SauWan gave birth to a daughter. The Mahs accepted their son-in-law for the sake of the grandchild and Mrs. Mah found a few good things to say about her daughter's husband. Two years later, she was bad-mouthing him again. "He beats my daughter. I've seen bruises on her. Now she won't let me in her house because her husband says I make trouble between them. It's not I who beats her! I'm going to find a *bomoh* to break the spell on her. I'm getting her away from that wife-beating two-legged snake!"

Whatever means she used, Mrs. Mah did succeed in getting SauWan to leave her husband. The next thing we heard was that SauWan had gone to study nursing in England. She never returned to Malaysia. Mother used this as a dire example of what could happen to us if we walked among the Malays.

* * *

Do not walk with Malays. Do not talk with Malays.

They are slothful; they make their women do all the work,
the growing of rice seed, transplanting the seedlings
to the watery fields, reaping the rice harvest, winnowing
the grain. They will kidnap girl children. They know magic . . .
one look in your eyes, a sprinkling of sand on your hand,
and you will follow them as in a dream.
Do not go among the Malays.

* * *

Our town was a microcosm of our society: Malays, the majority race in Malaysia, being half the population, tended to look for friends among their own race; ditto for the Chinese, who made up forty percent of the population. The Indians, being a very small minority, about eight percent, felt more at home with the Chinese, the other immigrant race. The sprinkling of Eurasians and Sikhs sought their friends among the Indians and Chinese.

Meanwhile, the Malays were told by their leaders that they had been, were being, robbed by the immigrant races; that the mineral wealth (tin) that rightfully belonged to them was being mined by interlopers. It became natural for them to distrust the immigrant races, especially the Chinese.

The Chinese and Indians were always conscious of the fact that they were immigrants and second-class citizens in their adopted country. In my early years, between 1946 and 1956, Chinese families were uprooted from their homes and resettled in 500 "New Villages" enclosed by high barbed-wire fences as part of the British colonial government's drive to wipe out communists who were guerrillas in the jungle. Many of these were Chinese. All Chinese were suspected of giving aid or of wanting to give aid to the communists.

In those days, the British practiced what they called the policy of "Divide and Rule." They favored the native race and fostered a climate of envy and distrust on all sides that eventually bore bloody fruit. At the time that they gave Malaya independence, in 1957, there was racial separateness but not animosity.

Under the leadership of our first prime minister, Tengku (Prince) Abdul Rahman, a gentle, tolerant, Oxford-educated Malay, the races lived fairly harmoniously together, and opposition parties were born. I remember being told to bring two dollars to school in 1963 to reserve a copy of *Time* magazine; the Tengku was to be featured on its cover as "Man of the Year" for his conception of a Malaysian federation of Malaya, Singapore, Sarawak, and North Borneo. I won a gold medal, First Prize, in the school's essay contest commemorating the formation of Malaysia with my mildly humorous depiction of the Tengku handing out cigars as excited "Father" of the new nation. Later, we were told that the special issue of *Time* was banned; our money was returned to us. The cover artist had depicted the Tengku rather unflatteringly and he was so furious at the "mockery" of him that he did not want anyone to see it.

The Chinese were urban, living in clusters of tin-miners' shacks that became towns; they were vegetable gardeners or shopkeepers or later, that hated thing, the "middlemen." The Indian immigrants, mostly from southern India, were unskilled labor who worked on rubber plantations, or educated Indians who dominated the clerical and skilled professions. Doctors and engineers were mainly Indians. The Malays were rural people, their occupations growing crops (bananas, sugarcane, coconuts) and fishing. By nature mild and peace-loving, they had a deserved reputation for gentleness and artistic talent. However, they were also known for "running amok," going berserk when overstressed. Any group of people, if told often enough they are victims, will eventually rise in rage to disprove that image.

Because the races kept apart, we remained unknown, alien to each other; unfounded rumors and political lies became legends and took on a vicious subterranean life in our minds. When we met, our prejudices formed a distorting glass wall between us. Racist perceptions strip away the freedom to be what you want to be; they reduce you to the lowest common denominator of your group; you have to struggle to recall that you are more than what the other sees.

There were not many Malay students in my school. Malay girls were mainly sent to parochial schools and educated in Malay, not English. The few students attending the Convent school were the daughters of civil servants or minor royalty. In 1957, the British passed all political power to the Malays and barred non-Malays from real power in the future: they wrote into the Malayan Constitution that only a Malay could be governor of a state or prime minister of the country. The Chinese had little interest in politics at the time and did not take part in the negotiations with the British.

Since Kelang was the royal town of the state of Selangor, the activities of the Sultan of Selangor often impinged on our daily lives. It was a fairly common thing for the newly built federal highway between Kelang and Kuala Lumpur to be closed for three hours by police whenever the Sultan wanted to race his foreign cars, a Jaguar, a Lamborghini, a Porsche. We would shrug and stay out of his way.

The royal household was always good for a bit of gossip. Everyone talked about the noisy fights the current Sultan had with his father, Sultan Hisamuddin Iskandar Shah, before the old Sultan died. The town gossips said it was because the old king's ghost was haunting the palace that the new sultan had to build a new *istana*. When the Sultan married a Minangkabau princess from Sumatra as his second wife and divorced the first wife to make her his Royal Consort, the gossips said it was a matter of her blood being bluer. When the official photograph of the new Sultana was available for purchase, it being mandatory for businesses to have photographs of the Sultan and his Consort on display, everyone speculated that the new Sultana must have used a love potion on him. The Minangkabau were famous as *bomohs*, witch doctors. Her Highness had a beautiful face but she must have weighed 200 pounds.

By law, Muslims are allowed four wives at a time and most of the nine sultans of the Malay states exercised this privilege quite vigorously. His Highness took a secondary wife when Her Highness was away on a three-month visit to her family in Sumatra. The new wife was a slim, sexy young Malay girl and it was obvious to everyone why he had married her. When Her Highness came home, the Sultan meekly divorced his new wife and sent her away. This happened more than once. Each time, the new wife was sent away when Her Highness returned. "Witchcraft!" the older people said, nodding their heads sagely.

I met the dragon-lady of Selangor when she interviewed and, subsequently, hired me to tutor her two daughters in English and mathematics. I had been recommended to her by my best friend's mother, Dr. L., who was physician to the distaff side of the royal household. Her Highness spoke excellent English, and asked intelligent and pertinent questions. She was gracious and I felt like something the cat had dragged in, standing on the opulent Persian carpet in a receiving salon. I was uncomfortable at being away from the familiar, the only Chinese among the alien people whom I had been taught to distrust and avoid all my life. I have no recollection of what answers I gave to make her believe I was competent enough to tutor her children. It was a most unnerving experience, complete with ladies-in-waiting who told me when to bow and when to back out of the royal presence.

For five months, before I went away to college, I rode my bicycle up to the new *istana* three time a week, and was let in the gate by the soldiers on guard. In addition to teaching eleven-year-old Princess Mariana and nine-year-old Princess Nohrani, the only children of the Sultana, I was also asked to teach fifteen-year-old Princess Fadzillah, a daughter of the divorced first wife. Princess Fadzillah was a beautiful girl with only two interests: which royal cousin she might marry and how to make herself more beautiful. Of my three charges, Princess Mariana was the best student, a serious girl wanting to please her mother in her studies. Princess Nohrani's attention had to be constantly recalled from eager discussion with Princess Fadzillah on the merits of Revlon versus Elizabeth Arden skin-care and cosmetics. She was always ready to encourage her half-sister's attempts to abandon the rules of English grammar for the rules of fashion and royal matches.

I hear the Princess Mariana is married and avoids publicity. Princess Nohrani, on the other hand, delights the gossips with her romantic escapades making the news every few years. Her third marriage reportedly involved a face-off between her father the Sultan and the Mentri Besar, the governor of Selangor. The governor was the sultan's age, and fully married (four wives). He divorced one to marry the princess. The Sultan finally consented to the marriage because the princess was carrying the governor's child. It was the scandal of the year. She is currently on her fourth marriage.

* * *

I will not read the newspaper. It is all bad news anyway.

I never worry about politics.
Nothing I do can make a difference.

The Malays own the country.
Keep your head down, don't attract their notice.
You will end up in Pudu Jail, disappear forever.

* * *

Malay is the language spoken in the market

In May of 1969, the racial tensions in the country were ruthlessly exploited by politicians to retain power for themselves. By 1968, the Chinese and Indians had become politically active and had formed political parties to oppose the dominant Malay party, the Alliance. In the 1969 elections, the Alliance won only a bare majority of the seats in Parliament. On May 13th, 1969, riots broke out in all the major cities: Kuala Lumpur, Penang, Ipoh, Johore Bahru. Rural

Malays, worked up to berserker rage by their leaders, were brought into the cities by the busloads, armed with *parangs*, long-bladed jungle cleavers, and ran amok. They slashed and chopped down Chinese in crowded places—markets, cinemas, bus stations, and main streets. After the first shock, the Chinese *tongs* armed their gang members and retaliated. Feisty Indians joined in the fighting on the side of the Chinese.

The government mobilized the army, which was predominantly Malay, declared a state of emergency, and clamped a three-day curfew on the country. This wave of rioting all over the country was carefully orchestrated anarchy for the political benefit of the ruling party, not a spontaneous outbreak of resentment as claimed by the government. The government declared the elections void. Many of the opposition party leaders were killed in the riots or arrested for fostering anarchy. The rest fled to Australia or Canada. Parliament did not meet again until 1971 and elections were not held again until 1974.

After the riots, the "Thirteen Articles of Sedition" bill was enacted as an amendment to the Malaysian Constitution. The bill defined thirteen topics banned from all discussion, chief of which were: Islam, the national religion; the political structure of the country; the Prime Minister; the rights of the Sultans and their royal houses; the economic and political situation of the different races; and the rights of *bumiputeras*. Stiff jail sentences were the punishment for violations of the Sedition Bill.

* * *

Don't talk about the Malays.
You never know who might be listening. Anyone can be an informer.

* * *

The fledgling free press, the "other English newspaper," the *Star*, was closed down. Chinese news presses were also closed by the government as fostering unrest. Malay newspapers were not subject to censorship. The only other newspaper unaffected was the *New Straits Times*, which had always been the official newspaper: it was funded by the government and under heavy censorship. International publications like *Time, Newsweek*, and the *Far East*

Economic Review were banned after the riots because their cover stories were: "Is Democracy Dead in Malaysia?" They carried full cov-
erage of the racial situation and the political implications of the
"spontaneous" riots. Naturally it became a point of honor for us,
non-Malay university students, to get our hands on a contraband
copy (smuggled in from Singapore) and to reproduce and dissemi-
nate as many copies of the forbidden articles as we safely could,
among our own immigrant people. The country was two enemy
camps now. The Malay students who had been our friends could not
bridge the huge divide between us. Those few who tried to talk to us
about the riots were viewed with fear and suspected of entrapment.
We became, overnight, truly paranoid.

Tengku Abdul Rahman had retired. The new prime minister,
Tun Abdul Razak, broadened the Alliance to include the remnants of
some opposition groups and changed its name to the National Front.
He introduced the New Economic Policy to encourage "fairer distri-
bution of wealth." Every company had to give a quota of their contracts to Malay companies. The University of Malaya, then the only
institution of higher education in the country, had to reserve one-
third of admissions for Malays, regardless of their test results. If
insufficient Malays were enrolled, those admissions stayed unfilled;
they could not be filled by qualifying non-Malays. The goal of parity
would be met by increasing the number of educated Malays or
decreasing the number of educated non-Malays.

My father got a Malay to agree to be his silent partner and obtained many contracts for supplies under the quota system using the
Malay's name as head of his company. He boasted that he would
often submit two contracts, one under his own name and one under
his Malay partner's, charging twice the prices he quoted under his
own name. His Malay bid always got the contract so he was making
twice the profit, even while paying a hefty kickback to his passive
partner. "I told you they're a lazy people," he said. "Ahmad could
be making all this money for himself if he wanted to. Instead he's
happy with the twenty-five percent I give him for letting me use his
name and doing nothing."

Most Malays associated with non-Malays only for business
purposes, believing the official explanation for the riots, feeling they
had to be loyal to the government and their leaders who had always
done things for the greater good of the Malays. To have tried to see
the non-Malay perspective would have been disloyal, *potong hidong*

rosak muka, "to cut off the nose to spite the face." Malays admire loyalty and bravery, be it in a man, woman, or animal. As witnessed by the memorial along the railroad tracks three miles outside the town of Teluk Anson: *There is buried here a wild elephant who, in defense of his herd, charged and derailed a train on the 17th day of September, 1894.*

On the evening of May 13th, 1969, I was eating dinner at my friend MeeChong's house in Petaling Jaya, a suburb of Kuala Lumpur. MeeChong's house was a few blocks from my rented room, near the university we both attended. Her father ran in, shouting, "Turn on the radio. Terrible things are happening in KL!" He had been listening to the six o'clock news on the radio. Mrs. Chew turned on the radio. The radio announcer's voice was high-pitched and excited. "I repeat, this is an emergency broadcast. Fighting has broken out along Batu Road, Ipoh Road, Campbell Road, Gurney Road, and other sections of the city. Do not go out. Stay home. We have no numbers at this time but our people report bodies littering the streets. The violence appears to have begun at the Federal and Cathay Cinemas where groups of *kampong* Malays are reported to have run amok with *parangs*. The estimated death toll at this time is at least two hundred. This is an emergency broadcast . . ."

My first thought was, "LeeLang is staying on Gurney Road!" My brother LeeLang was on a three-month training course at the Telecommunications Centre on Gurney Road. Then I remembered he was actually at the University Hospital visiting his fiancé, who had been admitted for minor surgery. I threw down my chopsticks with a rushed explanation to my hostess and jumped on my Honda 50, a used motorcycle LeeLang had bought for me with his first earnings when he graduated. I rushed to the University Hospital and was greatly relieved to find him at his fiancé's bedside. He had not heard the news and was about to drive back up to Gurney Road. We decided he should come to my lodgings until the rioting was over.

I do not normally listen to the news. I shudder to think what would have happened had MeeChong's father not been a news fanatic. My brother would have run right into the mobs had he gone back to Gurney Road unsuspectingly. He would have become a statistic of the riots. I would have become the only hope of the family for financial support and higher education for the younger siblings. I could not have married my husband; I would not have come to the

United States, and I would not have grown bold enough to write my uncensored thoughts or learned to think beyond my responsibility for the family's welfare and safety.

Three days later, the army had established control. The "amok" Malays had been bused back to their villages. The government lifted the curfew for one hour a day, gradually increased this to three, and finally lifted it altogether. Life slowly regained its normal surface rhythm but many previously peaceful "live and let live" Indians and Chinese bought long knives and hid them in their houses, so that they would not be totally helpless should another round of rioting break out again. Life regained its surface rhythm, but stories of personal tragedies seeped through the community like floodwaters, leaving residues of fear, loathing, and active distrust.

People living above the shophouses in Campbell and ChowKit roads swear this is true. The Malay soldiers would aim up at their windows when they peeped out and shoot off rounds of bullets. Their window shutters are riddled with bullet holes. Some of the bullets came through into the rooms and killed a baby. A woman had her eye shot out in another house.

Many people never came home that night. They are still missing. People by the river say they saw hundreds of bodies floating downstream. Govind, an Indian watchman at the General Hospital morgue, says the Malay soldiers took away bodies by the truckloads. He thinks they buried them secretly in a mass grave.

The Lees' daughter went to see a Chinese sword-fight movie, the afternoon matinee, at the Cathay Theater that day. She never came home. Mr. Lee went to look for her. He never came home. Mrs. Lee went out to look for him after the curfew was lifted. Her brothers say she was obsessed with the idea that her husband's and daughter's bodies were among the bodies floating in the river. They found her on the river bank. Her face was down in the water. She had drowned in six inches of water.

The Indian Chandra had no food in the house. He was desperate; his children were crying for food. He sneaked out to go to his brother's house to get food. He was shot by a soldier. Now his wife and children are crying for more than food.

Some of the stories were on a lighter note.

Mr. Chan heard the news at his office. He called his wife in the sub-urbs and told her that gangs of Malays were gathering in town with knives and there was a possibility of riots. He told her to run to the grocery store and stock up on necessities; he was coming home right away. By the time he got home, rioting had began and the shops had closed. He was dismayed to find that his wife had not bought food and rice as he expected. Instead, Mrs. Chan proudly showed him the thirty-six rolls of toilet paper she had bought on his instructions.

I was lucky my landlord had a huge bag of rice and canned goods in his house. I did not have any food except a loaf of bread and a jar of jam. Mr. Foo gladly shared his food with LeeLang and me. He did not feel as generous or sympathetic when the Malay neighbor, three doors away, came to borrow rice on the second day of curfew. He did give the *Inche* five *katis* of rice for his family, but he grumbled long about "feckless Malays. They know how to enjoy themselves singing and making their houses beautiful. But they don't know the first thing about being thrifty and saving. They never look ahead or prepare for bad days. Improvident, that's the Malays! They know no shame at all—they come begging for rice when their people are out there killing our people! They're lucky that I am a kind-hearted man and not vindictive at all."

In 1971, Joe and I spent the summer in Israel with his parents en route to the United States. Because I had no fixed ideas about Arabs, and they did not see me as enemy Jew, interacting with the Arabs I met in Hebron, Bethlehem, and Jerusalem was warm and without the distorting filter of racial fears. In fact, my mother-in-law once accused me of being an "Arab lover" for being more friendly toward them than to her Jewish friends. She was very upset by the fact that my Malaysian passport specifically forbade me to visit Israel. We had obtained a visa on a separate piece of paper from the Israeli Consulate in Singapore for my visit. "You are Jewish now! You should tear up that disgusting, anti-Semitic thing at once!" she said. "Please be reasonable," I said. "I am Malaysian; I need my passport to travel. Ripping it to shreds would not change my country's attitude toward Jews or Israel, and it would inconvenience me terribly." At this, she fell on my neck and cried that I would be a good wife for Joe, that I was a strong woman. My mother-in-law was a volatile person; one thing you could never accuse her of was that life was dull with her around.

During my visits home to Malaysia, I have noticed that racial tension is proportionately in reverse to the economic situation: when times are bad, people look for someone to blame, and they fall back on the most familiar scapegoat, the other race. In 1987, Prime Minister Tun Mahathir bin Muhammad had opposition leaders arrested, and suspended four newspapers to deflate rising tension between Malays and Chinese. When the economy is booming, as it is now, there is little tension; everyone is happy and disposed to see the good in others. I hope the economy will continue to be good, that education will increase tolerance and understanding between the races of Malaysia, and that politicians have matured enough to deal with problems through talking and negotiations, that they will never again need to resort to a solution like the May 13th killings. But I am not optimistic about the human race's ability to learn from history; especially now, in the aftermath of the O.J. Simpson trial, when racial divisiveness is more apparent than I have ever seen it in American society. The divisive trend of current social thinking along racial lines reminds me depressingly of the social climate in Malaysia before the May 13th, 1969 riots. I did not know to be apprehensive about large-scale racism and reverse racism before, but now I do; and I am afraid. The Malays have a proverb for this situation: "*Anjing galak, babi berani.* The dogs are fierce and the pigs daring; both sides are ready for battle and bloodshed."

At the university, I had been friendly on a professional basis with two poets who were Malays: Azahari Johari and Mohammed Haji Salleh. We could discuss anything to do with the arts or our writing. We avoided all talk of political or religious beliefs, even before the May 13th riots, before the Sedition Bill, partly because we knew there was no common ground to meet in those areas. True friendship is possible only between equals. Or two who perceive each other as equals. It was only after I left Malaysia and came to America that friendship with a Malay became possible. My very close friend of twenty-plus years is Rabitha, the Malay girl who married the previously mentioned Peace Corps volunteer, R.J. Because our husbands were good friends, we both shed our conditioning and grew to know, to love, and to trust each other. Away from the charged atmosphere of paranoia and racial distrust, of "dog eyes dog at the limited feeding bowl," I was able to interact easily and become friends with a few Malays who had also been transplanted to the United States and who had absorbed the Western idea of equals discussing ideas without feeling diminished or threatened by differences in opinion.

College Days (L to R): Myself with friends Edda da Silva (Indian), Ivy Goh (Chinese), and Abdul Wahid (Malay), on the University of Malaya campus in 1970

29

The Writing Life

I wrote my first poem in jest. My friend Susan had a cousin, Dennis, a boy our age who, in the manner of boys aged fifteen, showed interest in a girl by teasing and attacking everything she believed or held in regard. Not knowing enough about sports, his interests, I had no way of similar reprisal. I wrote a parody of Wordsworth's "Ode upon Westminster Bridge." My "Ode upon Dennis' Belly" was a mock-heroic sonnet on his physique. I laughed as I wrote it and it made Susan and even its victim laugh. Nana, grandmother to both, told me it was "wicked and clever," after she laughed over it. I gave the poem to Dennis and forgot about it. I did not write poems then and did not think of writing any more poems.

That was my final year in the Kelang Convent School. From the nuns, I went to Kuala Lumpur and had two years of pre-university education at St. John's Institution on Bukit Nanas (Pineapple Hill). St. John's was a boys' school and it had just become co-educational for its Sixth Form classes. I was one of twelve girls allowed on its male premises. It was a Catholic School run by Dominican monks. Brother Celestine, my English teacher, was an Australian. It was he who set me on the road to poetry with a class assignment: to write a poem. We all groaned and tried to talk him out of it. "We can't write poems!" we said. The boys were especially insulted—poetry was "sissy stuff" written by Victorians and dead men. Or half-dead men, anyway. Yew Kong, one of our star athletes, stole a goldfish from

Brother Celestine's aquarium and swallowed it before our shocked eyes, so that he could write a poem about something real and manly.

At the time, I was living in a rooming house with eight families. Mother had arranged for me to share a room with the landlady and her middle-aged daughter, Ah Chan (Pearl). Pearl and I shared a double bed and Old Mrs. Mow slept on the floor by the bed. Her four sons and their families had some of the other rooms and the rest she rented out to three other families. It was not a quiet house.

It was a rainy afternoon. I sat in the hall with children rolling marbles under my feet and tried to think poetic thoughts. I failed. Finally, I wrote a poem about the rain. I don't recall the poem except that I tried to capture the sound and tactile feel of hot tropical rain and how it made me feel. To my surprise, Brother Celestine praised it and read it to the class, who also liked it. Brother Celestine did not like Yew Kong's poem about how the goldfish felt as it was plucked from its watery tank and dropped into a man's red gullet. I did. I thought Kong's poem was funny. I see now that Brother Celestine had romantic ideas about poetry. But at the time, his praise made me realize I had enjoyed writing the poem though I did not think it was a very good poem. I had liked sorting through words in my vocabulary to evoke, with precision, what rain was and what I felt at that point in my life. I had liked placing words, like musical notes, next to one another, seeing how their sounds and connotations matched or clashed. I had liked putting into words what rain meant to me. It was something I had never thought about, something I took for granted like the air I breathed. I realized that writing poems was a concrete way for me to think about things. Writing poems was a way of recording my life, my mental development.

My early poems were like journal entries. And I was intoxicated with alliteration and big polysyllabic words, scattering them through my poems like a child showing off. Underlying them, a hunger for meaning—as evidenced by the early poem "Sunday."

Sunday

Saturday night's taste soured.
Waking up disgruntled by
the sun in my eyes;
my head hurts.

The sun's hot breath
fans my narcolepsy.
Yet another bath.
I sweat.

Ice cubes melt ineffectually,
tepid drinks
flat on the tongue.
I thirst.

The radio blaring earnestly
unintelligible noise.
Anyone listening?
My ears ache.

Sunset! Another Sunday going,
another endless day ended,
"Another step forward."
Where are we going?

Ants on a white-washed wall;
Meaningless movement
Empty existence;
Sunday to duller Sunday,
We are the Living?

—from *No Gods Today* (1969)

Edwin Thumboo, a professor at Singapore University, had
a poetry column in the Sunday cultural section of the *Straits Times*.
I sent the poem to him and he published it, pointing out its
faults and strengths as a guide to how poetry should be done. This
was my first published poem and it reinforced my desire to write
poetry.

Other early poems recorded discovery of self and the world. At
that time, I was very pessimistic about love and marriage.
Everywhere I looked, I saw unhappy couples and poverty that
scoured people raw and mean. Here's a stanza from an untitled
poem and the poem "Be Still My Soul," giving myself advice about
love.

The thump of the drum.
the blare of clarinets announce
the bride; cups clatter on thick
cheap porcelain saucers; weak
tepid tea flows sluggish, sluicing down
bananas and biscuits dry on the tongue.
The groom thinks bleakly of coming days
of marital bliss, plain rice and salted fish,
sliced with debts from the wedding dinner.
His parents beam over cups of bridal tea
And the iron sizzles
          On the pale banana leaf.

—from "Untitled," No Gods Today

Be Still My Soul . . .

Be still my soul, there is no love,
No bright foliage on green hills.
The brown cows have cropped all bare,
Leaving balls of prickly mimosa
And cloudy roses blooming in dung.
Be silent, love, there is none left
To call by that glad name;
Through the ages of deceit
We have bought flawed fragments
Of Happiness with counterfeit.
Beware, my heart, there is no joy
In love purchased at the high price
Of momentary self-deception,
Or in washing roses tarred with dung.
The petals come apart in our anxious hands.

—from No Gods Today

     There are only that many poems or years in which one can
indulge in despair at the human condition. I left Catholicism after I
found the father confessor displaying a little too much eagerness to
hear my sins against purity. At the time I attended St. John's
Institution, I was very devout, I went to 6 A.M. mass daily, and felt I

was a great sinner for having impure thoughts. In my first year at the University of Malaya, I read Sartre and Camus and fell in love with existentialism.

No Gods Today

The Chinese
Like St. Paul's Romans
to make sure
have many gods
many many gods . . .
I am Chinese
Born not bred
I have no gods.
Yesterday and the day before
I worshipped some god or other.
Today I rest.
Today I have no gods.
This day I eat, sleep, love or think I do,
Hate for spice, stir up a little wind
to rock a little the various altars
of godly people
safe in their closed brick cellars
Air-conditioned by faith and prayers.
I have no altars in
the huge house of my mind:
No stone gods
Wooden gods
Nor absent gods,
Only shadows that fade
Clays that crumble
Leaving on my empty hands
        a little grime
Flakes that join the doubt-dusted air.

—from *No Gods Today*

Poetry has affected my life in many ways. It has made me live with an enhanced awareness of the world and people around me, made me examine my life and experiences for meaning that I may learn from it and share it with others. It drastically changed my life in another way: poetry brought my husband to me. I met my husband, Joe Goldberg, because a friend gave him a copy of my first book of poems, *No Gods Today*. He liked it and asked to be introduced. We met, grew to love each other, and married. This brought me to America and brought me into the Jewish religion; both have been home to me since.

I developed a sense of humor from living with my husband and living in America. It took me ten years of "writer's block" silence to assimilate my adopted culture and to be able to write for and about it. I had not written about my Malaysian-Chinese heritage while I was in Malaysia, mainly because I had no occasion to think about it. Everyone knew what I knew; there was no reason to articulate the obvious. It was after I came to America and looked homeward with the eyes of the exile that I gained the perspective and the desire to write about growing up in Malaysia, the myths and gods my mother gave me, the effect my family and upbringing had on my character.

Had I stayed in my native land and raised my children there, I would have assumed they would absorb their cultural heritage from their environment. I would not have felt the need to write for them the cultural heritage that was my duty to pass to them. It was this need that moved me, with the birth of my youngest daughter, to write poems about growing up Chinese in Malaysia. From there, it was an inevitable step to writing poems celebrating people, in Malaysia and in the United States; to affirm the wonderful crazy-quilt qualities found in humanity everywhere. I stopped looking at the empty space above the water and focused on the water in the glass, instead.

30

A Retrospective Interview

In July 1995, Nor Faridah Abdul Manaf conducted an interview with me by correspondence for her Ph.D. research on Malaysian women writers of the 1960s and 1970s. Following are extracts from that interview.

Please furnish me with some details of your background, grow ing up in Malaysia: birthdate and place, education, family, life as a student at MU [the University of Malaya].

I was born on August 20th, 1946 in the royal town of Kelang, Selangor, Malaya—delivered by a midwife at home. This was short-ly after the end of the Japanese occupation and British troops had returned to Malaya. My mother says she was able to get condensed milk to feed me. This may be why I do not have a liking for sweets or desserts—I had an overdose of sweetness at babyhood. I grew up with a large family, I was the second child of six, and the oldest daughter.

I had a year of kindergarten Chinese in a parochial school. Then I was sent for English medium education (primary and sec-ondary to Form Five) at the Kelang Convent School, where Irish nuns were my role models. In 1964–1966, I attended Form Six (Upper and Lower) at St. John's Institution on Bukit Nanas in Kuala Lumpur. During 1967–1970, I majored in English Literature at

Universiti Malaya. I graduated with Bachelor of Arts, Upper Class Honors. I did a semester in the Diploma of Education but switched to post-graduate work in American Literature when I was offered a tutorship (teaching assistantship) in the English Department. I did not complete the Master's degree as I met and married my husband and left for America in 1971.

Student life at Universiti Malaya was exciting. I began to think for myself, to question the docile role which I was raised to play. Here I met older students, people like Shirley Lim and Tina Chin, unconventional and colorful and outspoken women who behaved as if they felt themselves equal to the male students and lecturers. Here I met older male students like Patrick Yeoh and Paul Yeow who had lived in England for teacher training, and who were no longer in awe of, or believed in, "the white man's superiority." They debated on equal standing with our English and American professors. The books I had access to in the university library (Sartre, Camus, existentialist writings) made me question the religion I had adopted (Catholicism) after years attending the Kelang Convent school. I had long ago given up on the Chinese gods as being too simplistic, bureaucratic, and fallible like humans. I converted to Judaism upon marriage and have been a conservative Jew since.

I had been raised to "never attract the attention of gods or government; consequences are always bad." When a picture of me on the Speaker's Stone in front of the MU Library was featured in the *Straits Times*, my parents were frightened out of their slippers, worried I would lose my federal grant money (I went to MU on a Teaching Scholarship). I had to promise them I would not orate on the Speaker's Stone again. This made me think about principles, ideals, and personal courage, how much of each did I have and what weighed more with me. I realized I was significantly lacking in courage and needed to work on that and on clarifying to myself what I believed in, what principles I would be willing to cowardly yield under pressure, and which were worth suffering for. This was the time I became active in molding my own character and personality.

What is your marital status? The number of children and their ages?

I married Joseph Ray Goldberg, a Jewish American, in February 1971; I converted to Judaism; and we have three daughters raised in the Jewish faith: Ilana Pu-Ying Goldberg, born in 1976; Shoshana

Mei-Ying Goldberg, born in 1977; and Rebecca Su-Ying Goldberg, born in 1980.

When did you first write?

I began writing poems when my Form Six English teacher, Brother Celestine, set our class a poetry writing assignment, and he especially liked the poem I wrote (a simple lyric poem on rain). I found that I liked the "centering" quietude of the creative process, the control and shaping of thought I reached in examining my life, the world, and people around me. I felt most alive when I was writing. So I kept on writing.

Who were your mentors where writing is concerned?

By mentors, do you mean living persons I learned from or writers whose work influenced me? I did not have any particular living mentor apart from Brother Celestine, my Form Six English teacher whose praise and delight in my first poems gave me confidence in myself and reinforced my desire to keep on writing. His tastes in poetry were the conventional: Romantic poets à la Keats, Wordsworth, and nature poetry, something I was not particularly drawn to. I write about nature as a metaphor for life and people. People (the socio-psychological and cultural workings of) are what I am compellingly intrigued by.

The poets whose work I especially admired at the time were T. S. Eliot, W. B. Yeats, e. e. cummings, Emily Dickinson, Po Chu-I, and Li Po.

Why do you write? Why poetry? Have you tried other genres? Please list published works. I am focusing on works written while you were in Malaysia.

"I think, therefore I am"—René Descartes. I write to think. The act of writing is my way, through the art of language, of discovering, of finding shape and meaning in my life, my experiences, the chaotic and apparent meaninglessness/futility of living. I write poetry because it is the most packed and effective medium for communicating feeling fused with thought and achieves that effect subtly, almost metaphysically. I have a perverse dislike of being told things. I like to see and arrive at ideas/meanings. I like saying things without saying them, if you follow me. This may be a result of my Chinese-Malaysian cultural upbringing. As to other genres, I occasionally write short stories, when the material I am interested in does not fit into the terse density of a poetic vignette. The following were published in University of Malaya journals between 1967 and 1969: "The Discovery" (*LIDRA*), "Unclean" (*LIDRA*), and "Unborn Tomorrow" (*The Annual Non-Hostelites Magazine*). I have also done a first draft of a fantasy novel and a collection of short stories, which I plan to work on further.

Were you conscious of writing as a woman back in the 1960s in Malaysia?

I knew the thoughts and reactions I had and that I wrote about were female, but not feminine per se. I was aware that I did not have a "conventionally feminine" mind. My mother used to lament the fact that I seemed to behave and think more like a boy than a girl when I was young. I admit I was guilty of male envy—I wanted the freedom that our society gave men, but not women. The freedom to be fully themselves, not compressed, squeezed tightly into molds, like the bound feet of my grandmother's generation. I felt constricted. I wanted to learn what sort of person I could be, if free to explore all the interesting paths marked "not for women," "not for sensible Chinese who must focus on earning money and giving their parents grand-children and filial piety." I wanted to be free to do and think and be. And I wanted to write about all of the process, the discovery, the being alive, as stated in the end couplet from the poem "For Edda":

> And we shall dance together when the rains come,
> Our glad voices filling the rain-dampened sky

I think the poem "Spider on a Wall of Sky" better states the reason I write:

> I have to find myself again
> And spin again my web,
> To give pattern to my existence.

Read "words" for "web" and "meaning" for "pattern." That was why I wrote in the early period of my writing life.

These days, those basic reasons for writing still hold true for me. But my aims have grown—I write to lead an examined life, to not simply exist without thought. I also write to celebrate life, the wonder of people, and nature and the miracle of being alive. I write to preserve my cultural heritage, to pass it on to my children and future generations; I hope my poems become bridges of understanding between peoples for we are all sisters and brothers under the skin. To make connections—in hopes that a reader somewhere, sometime, will feel less alone in reading one of my poems. We all have similar hopes, dreams, pain and sorrow, and losses, in our life cycles. Knowing someone has felt this too, helps give us strength to endure, to go on.

How did you make time to write?

In the early years, easily. As a student, undergraduate and post-graduate, I had an amazing amount of time for writing, compared to life as a full-time mother and homemaker, part-time creative writing teacher, and volunteer in my synagogue community and the writing community. These days I have to struggle to get time to write as I'm a Director on my Synagogue Board, President of my Synagogue Sisterhood, poetry editor for *Potomac Review,* and a director of the Word Works, a non-profit small press in Washington, D.C.

I think you were very conscious of environmental issues even way back in the 1960s. I thought "Paper Boats" reflected your environmental concerns. Are there any more pieces like that?

In the 1960s, the environment was something we all took for granted; we never gave it a thought as being a non-renewable resource. In the poem "Paper Boats," I was actually more concerned with people as a resource that was profligately being wasted, taken for granted, being made to fit into little slots mandated by family and society, not allowed to fulfill their potential. The boat was a metaphor for people. The trash dump came in as a means of showing how wasteful we are of each other's lives, loves, and caring. I was a deep pessimist at the time about marital relations. All I saw were unhappy marriages, men being free to have secondary wives, women trapped and constricted in the roles society approved for them. It seemed to me at the time that callous husbands, despotic fathers, unwanted pregnancies, and fickle lovers were the fundamental conditions of being female.

I think you were quite preoccupied with themes of identity search, futility, child-parent relationships, love and letting go of the past, and so on. Would you like to add more?

Your discernment of themes in my early work is very good. In addition, I would say I was concerned with social realism (see the poems "Asian Child," "Shame," and "The Pawnbroker's") and marital bleakness. My thoughts and writing were permeated by a fatalistic view of life, an aching awareness of the transience of life, of love, and the awareness that to live, to love, is to suffer. I tended, and still do, to equate living with loving; to live is to love—family, mate, children, friends. To live without loving is to live only for oneself and then what are we? Another example of the transience of life theme is from the poem "Eugenia," published in the *Annual Non-Hostelites Magazine* in 1968:

Evergreen is the leaf of finding
the truth that living is dying,
Growing is decaying.
And Fear, taloned, claws
long fine scratches
In the quick of our flesh.

The poem "With a Sigh," also in the same magazine, has this theme or what you could call futility. I think of it as a questioning for meaning: why do we suffer?

With a Sigh

Trees rot
Flowers fade
Grasses die
With only a sigh
To show their passing

Men love
Hearts break
People weep
they all will sleep
the sleep that knows no waking
Hens squawk
Babies wail
Between birth
and a bed of earth
there is an interim called life

A life filled
With pain and grief
So we cry
we know not why
and we live—with a sigh
        with a sigh

The poem "Sitting in Grass" is a bit puzzling. It reminds me of "Daffodils" by Wordsworth. This talk of a young woman discovering her female body is indeed ahead of its time (considering it was written in the 1960s). I mean I know then women were busy burning their bras but really, were you affected by the women's movement then to have written this piece?

Sitting in Grass

Sitting in grass
I watch a beetle rise
along a *lallang* leaf
And as I bite my nails,
I wonder at the hair on my arms.
I wonder also at the hair
on blades of grass, the furtive silence
of birds in bushes.
And as I touch the skin on my thighs,
Young as the petal of a rose,
a bubble of wonderment grows
and grows, permeating me

with the warmth of the sunlight I watch,
liquid on palm fronds.

—from *No Gods Today*

I think the women's movement definitely shows its influence here.
While I was disapproving of the waste of bra-burning, besides thinking it an exhibitionistic activity (the bras that were in the newspapers
being DD cup sizes and I felt that those bras were mainly functional).
I could see burning padded bras that turned women into male fantasy figures. But not wholesale bra discarding. I am a moderate femi-
nist today—believing that women should have equal opportunities
as men, equal remuneration for their equal work, etc. But I do not
agree in principle with the trampling down and belittlement of men
to empower women. As with any crusade for change, however,
extremists are prolific and necessary to succeed, sadly enough. I
wrote "Sitting in Grass" in a moment of discovery of self and I liked
the poem then and today still, as a protest against the taboo against
self-examination, the unspoken social rule that women should not be
proud of, or take pride in, their bodies feeling alive. I had a lump in
my breast and, when I saw a doctor about it, I remember my appalled
embarrassment and indignant denial when she asked me if I examined my breasts often. The idea of touching one's own body was
taboo in the 1960s. Now, women know it is false modesty, and that
breast examination is a vital precaution against breast cancer.

*You seem to speak of sexual harassment (unwanted attention) in
"Doppelganger." What triggered it? How do you explain the poem on the
golden girl, Dorothy?*

Doppelganger

As I pace through dazed corridors,
a stranger laughs, stubbing out his cigarette
on the bumper of my car,
and slowly follows,
his shadow moving with my shadow.
Watching the slow curve of my eyes
he tangents a smile.

I quicken my pace.
Reaching high ground, I pause,
forgetting him in the immensity of sky.
Standing in the wind, body remembers soul
flickering with blown bougainvilleas,
then lost in the indifferent white
      of a passing cloud.
I return to my valley roads
where the stranger stands, waiting.

                        —from *No Gods Today*

Actually, though it reads like it is about sexual harassment, the poem is on one level about mental depression, the darker side of ourselves, from which we can escape only temporarily. On another level, it could be about a husband and wife relationship, of spousal abuse, for the "I" of the poem must "return to my valley roads/ where the stranger stands, waiting." No matter how well we think we know our spouses, sometimes they say or do something that drives home how little we really know their inner selves. They are familiar strangers.

To Dorothy—Poem for a Golden Girl

In deepest gloom, I come to you
weighed down by the shadows
of dark thoughts and melancholy.
And you are there
with your laughter and bright eyes.
The gold of your laughter
threads my songs with beauty
and shadows vanish in your presence.
I'll remember the sparkle,
the warmth of your friendship
in the nights of my life.

     I wrote this simple poem to celebrate a friend's sister. Dorothy was a delightful extrovert, vital, glowing, zestful, always vibrant and talkative. She was so enthusiastic and energetic, she made even speculation about the weather fun. She was like a lamp, with a bright flame within. I have not seen Dorothy these 25 years but I hear from my friend that she is married with two children and grown fretful with worries and life. I am sorry to hear that. No mystery here. A simple poem for a lovely person. I admired her because I was the opposite of Dorothy; I was quiet, dreadfully introverted, and often depressed in those days. I seldom said what I thought except on paper, never held up my end of an interesting debate or conversation. My then boyfriend was an artist and he used to berate me for this; he was a fiery cockerel and loved arguing for argument's sake, often switching sides just to keep a debate alive. "I don't think fast on my feet," I said, in excuse. But it was and is the truth. When it comes to ideas, I do not think fast. I come to ideas and their articulation by way of metaphor and connotations/associations, by sensibility, not reason, not by rational $e=mc^2$.

I am a bit dazed by your piece called "Even the Waters . . ." Perhaps this indicates my lack of knowledge regarding certain Christian connotations. But the theme of futility is back again. Am I wrong to assume this?

from **Even the Waters**

> *the flood breaketh out of the inhabitant; even the waters forgotten of the foot: they are dried up, they are gone away from men.*
>
> —The Book of Job, Chapter 28, Verse 4

Rain on a window pane:
the sifted light settles softly
in the darkened room.
The cat snoozes, curled in a warm ball
Its tail twitches in an effort
to touch the rims of a dream.
The whole house is silent
with the unresenting silence
of rain-flooded grass . . .

Time sleeps . . . and dreams . . .

    many dreams

till yesterday mingles with tomorrow
and today is a watery blob on a bare table.
Tomorrow and today and the day before
run into each other, the drifting
leaves of a Chinese calendar
slow blackening, slow burning in one fire.

In the time-forgotten temple
the yellow-faced monk sits
cleaning the altar. He carefully
washes the gods' faces, puts
new clothes on their clay bodies.
The Chinese nun sits and collects money
after reading each fortune.
In the outer hall, many wait
to know their past and future,
their interest is mainly monetary too.
The monk's daughter plays hop-scotch
in the third hall; she is convent-educated
and plans to become a Catholic.
The waters of baptism break over the font . . .

Each morning they come, the diabetics
for their insulin injection.
Patiently they wait, a line of flabby women.
When it is finished, half the morning gone,
they take a bus home and recount
to uninterested housemates the sagas
of friends they met that day.
Alone, aging with no other programs,
they make their daily pilgrimage,
drift past other diabetics on similar voyages,
their anchor a bus-stop sign.

An old man said, "Time is a bus."
An old man sits under a tree
watching the cows graze.
An old man sits under the grass.
He watches the cows climb the stars.
He watches time pass.

In the cemetery the quiet house
listens to silence after the rain,
listens to echoes of violin songs
lingering in earth-polished skulls.
Sleeping in darkened rooms, they hear
the silence of rain and death,
                and time slumbers.

—from *No Gods Today*

Perhaps if I say right off that the "quiet house" of the poem is the
grave, things will fall into place for you. The quotation from the
Book of Job gives the poem its theme: Why has God abandoned
mankind? Why are our lives full of suffering? We, no matter our different hopes, dreams, are all marching to Time's drumbeat toward
the grave, the quiet house where we "hear / the silence of rain and
death, / and time slumbers." We don't have to keep going when we
are dead. Remember I was raised in a culture that emphasized the
clan, not the individual, where the work ethic and being a good little
worker ant in the anthill was the raison d'être (this was not enough
for me), where the pursuit of personal happiness was considered
selfish and unfilial.

What's your immediate concern now where writing is concerned?

My concerns have always been with people, and the meaning we
need to give our lives. What makes life worthwhile for us? How do
people forge strong souls and character in the sandstorm of being in
decaying bodies, subject to illness and disease as we are, subject to
chance encounters with muggings, rapists, accidents like mudslides,
earthquakes, subject to losses of all we treasure, loved ones, health,
jobs, and so on? I write to record the times I am living in, the social
and emotional soul of our present society. We are so vulnerable and
puny yet we build and build, river-spanning bridges, homes, have
children, fall in love, give hostages to fortune. People are wonderful!
And funny! And amazing! I write to celebrate them.

   Life is full of griefs. But we try, we live as fully and lovingly as
we can, as generously, in spirit and community works, as we can;
we should respect others' rights to be different. The process itself is
the reward.

About the Author

Hilary Tham was born in Kelang, Malaysia. She has at various times been a tutor to princesses, an insurance-claims reviewer, and vice-president of her synagogue, but she has always been a poet. Published in Malaysia, Singapore, New Zealand, Israel, and the United States, she is author of *No Gods Today* (1969), *Paper Boats* (1987), *Bad Names for Women* (1989), *Tigerbone Wine* (1992), and *Men and Other Strange Myths* (1994). She has been featured often on National Public Radio and Radio Pacifica.